HOW TO BUY A
HOME IN IRELAND

A GUIDE TO NAVIGATING THE
IRISH PROPERTY MARKET

In 2019, teacher Ciarán Mulqueen began the process of buying a home in Ireland. Over a year-long search, as he became more and more disillusioned with the difficulties of the market here, he decided to create an online community where people could share their experiences of buying a property – and so the social media powerhouse Crazy House Prices was born.

Three years later, with over 120k+ followers across social media accounts, Crazy House Prices is the first port of call for home-buyers as ordinary purchasers and industry experts come together to share their tips, information and experiences, good and bad, of buying a home in Ireland.

Ciarán is a regular contributor on radio and TV and the host of a popular podcast giving tips and insights into the Irish property market. He lives in a renovated and retrofitted 100-year-old home with his wife and daughter in Dublin.

HOW TO BUY A HOME IN IRELAND

A GUIDE TO NAVIGATING THE IRISH PROPERTY MARKET

Ciarán Mulqueen

HACHETTE
BOOKS
IRELAND

First published in Ireland in 2023 by
HACHETTE BOOKS IRELAND

3

Cataloguing in Publication Data is available from the British Library

ISBN 9781399716925

Typeset in 12pt Lato by Cathal O'Gara

Printed and bound in Great Britain by
Clays Ltd, Elcograf S.p.A.

Hachette Books Ireland policy is to use papers that are natural, renewable
and recyclable products and made from wood grown in sustainable forests.
The logging and manufacturing processes are expected to conform to the
environmental regulations of the country of origin.

Hachette Books Ireland
8 Castlecourt Centre
Castleknock
Dublin 15, Ireland

A division of Hachette UK Ltd
Carmelite House, 50 Victoria Embankment, London EC4Y 0DZ

www.hachettebooksireland.ie

CONTENTS

Permission acknowledgements

1. Massive thank you to my followers and staff in EBS for sending me the tips on what to do before building your home.

2. The Competition and Consumer Protection Commission (CCPC) for providing the questionnaire on how to choose the right solicitor.

3. Revenue.ie and the Local Authority Home Loan website for information on government schemes in Chapter 7.

Information is up-to-date as of January 27th 2023.

Note from author

Please note: I am not a qualified financial advisor. Any financial tips in this book are what worked for me, but please seek professional advice from a qualified financial advisor. All interest rates were correct at the time of writing, however these are changing very regularly. There are mortgage calculation tools available for free on ccpc.ie to keep up to date on the most recent mortgage interest rates.

For my dad, Brendan Mulqueen, who was my biggest supporter in everything I did, no matter how bad I was at it. I know he would be proud of me and my family, and I miss him every day.

INTRODUCTION

MY name is Ciarán Mulqueen and I am the creator of the CrazyHousePrices social media accounts. I started the page in 2019 when my wife Melissa and I were about a year into our own home-buying journey, which we have just completed (including a full renovation of a 100-year-old house). The page has consumed large parts of my life over the last three years, becoming a bit of an obsession for me, but a great one. The page has built an incredible community and I am very proud of it and passionate about it.

I have learned so much from this community and I have had, quite literally, tens of thousands of conversations with all sorts of people, including professionals involved in the home-buying process. This means I know exactly what problems people are facing. I like to think of it as collaborative research, 90,000 (at the time of writing) like-minded individuals sharing their learnings, experiences and problems.

Buying a home in Ireland is, at present, very difficult. Unnecessarily difficult, in my opinion. Which is why I wrote this book. I want to make it easier for you to find and buy your home by sharing with you a collection of the best tips that I have learned over the last few years.

My aim with this book is to organise all of this information for you into one place that is easy to understand and enjoyable to read. Basically, this is the book I wish had existed when I started my own home-buying journey. Good luck and happy house hunting!

Ciarán Mulqueen

January 2023

OUR STORY

OUR story is one like many others; a story of frustration and desperation in our effort to find a home in what is the most chaotic period ever in Irish housing. When myself and my wife Melissa began our search for a home in 2018, we did not anticipate how difficult it would be to buy a home in Ireland. Nor did we realise just how awful the value for money was. We were fortunate enough to be able to live in Melissa's family home, which is in Portobello in Dublin. We wanted to buy a house somewhere within 10 to 15 minutes of there to try and stay close to both of our families.

So, for the first time, I took an active interest in finding out what was for sale nearby. The Daft app has a handy feature where you can 'search nearby' to find homes for sale around you. One of the first that caught my eye (for the wrong reasons) was 19A Long Lane in Dublin 8. This house was the muse for my Instagram page. It is my first ever post and it quickly got a lot of attention. The house is known as Ireland's skinniest house and is a mere 180 centimetres wide and 34m². It was for sale for €265,000 (I don't think it ever sold). I was shocked at how little you got for your money in Dublin, especially compared to elsewhere in Ireland and even other European cities. I quickly noticed a trend of absurdly high house prices, often for houses that needed a huge amount of work to bring them up to modern standards.

We only ever looked at existing houses; we couldn't find any 'new-builds' in the areas we were looking at for less than €750,000. We booked a series of viewings, which back in 2019 was an easier task than it became shortly after. Estate agents became overrun with not just enquiries, but offers, sometimes from individuals who had not yet ever set foot in the property.

Having begun the viewing process, we found quite a few houses that we really liked. There was one in Chapelizod that stole a piece of our hearts. It had the most incredible garden. The foot of the garden had a small deck overlooking

4

the Liffey, with its own little jetty for a boat, a true city oasis. There's a post about it on my page, but it didn't have any parking, and offers fast began to soar, so we never put in an offer. I do however still think about that house all the time. I think it sold for close to €500,000 in the end – out of reach.

We viewed more houses, and eventually started placing bids on homes that we didn't love, but would do us for our needs. We were realising that we might not be able to find our 'dream home' after all. (I have always hated this saying; if your dream home is a three-bed semi-d, your dreams aren't big enough!)

Having lived in Dublin 8 for quite some time, the area had become home for us. It was hard to imagine not walking the same routes, no longer being close to family, not visiting the same local cafés and shops and no longer being a short walk from the city centre. One area in particular had made its way to the top of the list: the Tenters. Situated at the heart of all that had become so important. It's a ten-minute walk from Melissa's parents' house and the same to work for me.

A few weeks before Christmas that year, we had seen a house that was for sale in the area and had fallen in love with it. We did what I tell everyone not to do: we got attached to it. We pictured ourselves living there, the adaptations we'd make to create our home, continuing to enjoy the local community we knew and loved, and starting our family. Our hopes were high. We put an offer in within hours of viewing it but were outbid within a week. We were devastated. This was the final straw for us and we decided to press pause.

I was 34 when we managed to buy our home; my parents had four children and were on to their third home by that age. Statistically (as proven by Dara Turnbull, research coordinator at Housing Europe) it is more difficult for this current generation to buy a home than any generation before. Because of this, I had to figure out a way to be successful. I love problem solving, and our problem was being outbid in bidding wars. It was then that we decided to try the off-market approach, as a last hope. My solution was to try and skip the bidding wars altogether and go directly to the vendors who were thinking of selling their home but had not yet approached an estate agent.

We loved the Tenters and decided to focus most of our letters there, with a handful dropped in on another road we loved slightly further afield. We posted about a dozen letters to houses we liked and some that looked vacant. We dropped them directly into the letterboxes. I used Google Maps to identify houses that suited our needs, ones with extensions already built, and gardens. We had nothing to lose. Having heard nothing back after a couple of weeks, we decided we would try again next year and hopefully prices would have come down by then. (They didn't, they went even higher.) Then we got the email ...

It came from the owners of the house next door to the one we had been outbid on. We could not believe it. Out of respect for that family's privacy, I won't go into the details they supplied, but it was a straightforward email saying that they had received our letter, that they were planning on selling the house soon and wanted to know if we would like to come and view it.

We knew already that we would love it given our attachment to the house next door. This house was an even better fit for us as it already had a small extension. When we visited, we were warmly welcomed by the owners, who turned out to be incredibly nice people. They were generous with their time and knowledge. They told us stories about growing up in the home, who the neighbours were, what factories and shops used to be nearby and all that had happened in the locality. We got a strong sense of how special this house was to them. It was clear it had been a happy home since the day it was built and had become their family home, remaining in the family for almost 100 years. It all felt right, if a little surreal. We adored the house.

Conveniently, it had already been valued and the valuation was the exact figure we had to spend. We agreed on that price that night and have been pinching ourselves ever since.

If you have followed my Instagram page at all, you will have heard about our 'letter trick' for buying our home off-market. It is not a trick at all, but that is the title my followers have given our approach.

We were fed up with losing out on homes we were bidding on and had reached a point where we were going to give up and try again within a year. This is a common story, and a feeling many people are familiar with. There is a sense of hopelessness at times, and you begin to feel like you will never own your own home. There are unspoken consequences to this; people delay life milestones, like starting a family, because they cannot rent or buy their own home. It is absolutely desperate and something that does not get enough attention.

THE TRICK

WE had all but given up on our home-buying journey. We had full mortgage approval and a guarantee of a 4.5x exemption (one of the benefits of being teachers with permanent jobs). Exemptions are explained in the next chapter. We had a very good deposit saved, thanks to both of us living at home for the previous few years and then Melissa's parents allowing us to live together in their home to save even more. We knew exactly how much money we had to spend on a home and how much we would have left over for renovations. We could find plenty of homes that we liked and were within budget, but we kept getting outbid.

Because our budget was relatively small for Dublin, we were looking at 'fixer-uppers'. Homes in good locations but requiring some (or a lot of) work. Anything turn-key was out of our reach and were often going well above their asking prices. There were no new-builds available and any fixer-uppers we were interested in were going above what we felt they were worth or that we could afford.

I had been suggesting to Melissa for months that we should write a letter, print off lots of copies and post them in letterboxes around areas we wanted to buy in. Just a simple letter explaining our story and offering people a market-value sale without the hassle and fees associated with using an estate agent. So, that's what we did. And it worked!

🏠 Good news story

33 and a single first-time buyer, I saved for years, living in Dublin and was looking for a house outside of it. I found my dream house but it was already sale agreed. It was a three-bed bungalow, no major work to be done and 1.1 acres of land. I used your page for tips, sorted out the application and paperwork needed, went with a broker for the mortgage and got approved. Three months later the house went back on the market. I rang straight away on February 11th, viewed it on the 13th, made an offer on the 15th and

---

got into a bidding war with another buyer. So, I sent a letter to the vendors, again on advice from your page, and I went sale agreed for asking price. Got my keys in September and couldn't be happier. I had followed your page for ages and actually messaged you on occasion for advice and you got back straight away. Your page and good news stories give people hope and independent advice without a sales pitch. Really, well done, Ciarán. Keep doing what you're doing.

Robyn, Laois

THE LETTER

It is worth stating that this will obviously not work for everyone. It will require you getting lucky, but it worked for us and I have been told by around 25 Instagram followers now that it worked for them also. Melissa wrote a nicely worded letter explaining our situation and a few other pertinent details. I won't put our exact letter in this book but here is a template that you might find useful. I would recommend making it your own and customising it however you feel will work best.

1. **Be polite.** You do not mean to cause insult or offence

but you are struggling to find a home due to the housing crisis.

2. **Be personable.** Explain your situation, that you are a first- or second-time buyer with fully underwritten mortgage approval.

3. **Be human.** Explain why you love the area and want to live there. We mentioned we were from the area, that I work in the local school and that we wanted to live close to our parents as we were looking to buy a family home and start our own family.

4. **Be useful.** Explain how you can offer a hassle-free, full-market-value sale and that the home will continue to be loved by a family or a single person who wants to become part of the community.

5. **Be profitable.** Explain how the seller could benefit from less hassle with viewings, from having to clean the home for photos and could also save on estate agents' fees (usually 1 – 2 per cent) plus other fees.

6. **Be convenient.** Sign off and mention that if they are thinking of selling their home in the foreseeable future, you would love it if they kept you in mind.

> ### 🏠 Good news story
>
> We were the first bidders on our house and were outbid within the week so we gave up. I remember telling a colleague that we were going to hold off for another few months before we looked again as we were heartbroken. Fast forward an hour later, the estate agent called and said the owners wanted to give it to us even though it was €5,000 less, because we had written a letter. In my letter I said we would look after the house and hopefully raise our kids there and I think that tugged on their heart strings. We are in now two months and absolutely loving it.
>
> *Jennie, Dublin*

There are some things you need to keep in mind when trying this approach. You need to make sure your letter is sensitively written. Imagine how you would feel if you received a note like this. Would you be happy to receive such a letter? Don't engage in this tactic unless you can promise a hassle-free, quick sale. Make sure that your mortgage is fully approved and underwritten, that you can definitely afford the market value of the home, and that you have everything you need in place (solicitor, surveyor, etc). Do not post letters in houses you know you cannot afford. Do your research on prices for the area. I recommend not putting any figures in your letter. If you are successful, the value will be decided by a valuer.

We posted our letters on roads we loved and kept a lookout for homes that might be vacant. If you're lucky and have local knowledge of the area, you could find a house that is about to go on the market. Friends may hear of people in that locality who are considering selling. The key here is getting the house before it goes to an estate agent.

⚷ Top tip

I often hear from my Instagram followers that they have used this approach when bidding on a home (a regular home on the market that is for sale with an estate agent). They explain that they wrote a letter to the vendor and this resulted in the vendor accepting their offer over someone else's. This is a risky move, as you may annoy the estate agent by going behind their back, or the vendor by sending them the letter when they have outsourced the sale of their home to the agent. Lots have had success with it, but I'm sure lots of others have not. I will leave this one up to you and your own judgement.

What happens if you're successful?

If, like us, you get lucky and someone is willing to sell you their home directly, the rest of the process is similar to any other sale of a property. The vendor will have the house valued and you can agree on a price together. The solicitors will do the rest. There is no booking deposit required. You must do the usual 'sale-agreed' steps (detailed in Chapter 14): employ your required professionals, have the bank valuation done, and so on.

Remember, and this is important: the sale is not final until both sides sign the contracts. Both seller and buyer can pull out of the sale at any time until then.

If you do go down this route and are successful, please do get in touch with me and let me know. I absolutely love hearing these stories!

ACTION STEPS

- Write your letter and identify areas in which you wish to post them.
- Make sure you have researched the values of the homes in the area so that you know you can afford the one you are interested in.

2

SIX MONTHS BEFORE APPLYING

WHAT YOU'LL NEED

- Your credit report
- Your savings plan
- Organised bank accounts

THESE six months are really important for getting yourself organised. When you're applying for a mortgage, six months is usually the minimum a lender will look back at. Depending on how the mortgage lending market is at the time of your application – for example if interest rates are going up and lenders are under pressure to be more strict with their lending – they may want to look back even further. So, it's wise to be organised. In this chapter I will run through everything you need in terms of documents, expectations and habits.

If you get organised now, future you is going to be very

happy. Even if, like me, you're not the type of person who is usually organised, it's time to change that. Buying a home is likely to be the most expensive purchase of your life, so it is worth the effort of changing habits if needed. These habits are easier to keep once you establish them, and will be very beneficial if you ever want to switch your mortgage, sell your home, or deal with any other things life throws your way.

For example, a challenge for us was that we get our payslips posted out to us each fortnight in paper form. My wife and I are teachers and the Department of Education wastes millions of euros per year doing this and no one knows why they won't switch to electronic payslips. So, we got ourselves a little filing cabinet and organised it with labels for each section: banking, insurance, payslips, marriage certificate, and so on. Keeping the payslips in the right order now will save you hours of hassle and stress down the line trying to find them all and put them in chronological order. Because we had our little filing cabinet, it saved us a lot of hassle and very much decreased the likelihood of arguments over who left what where.

⊶ **Top tip**

You'll read a lot in this book about needing a 10 per cent deposit to buy your home. I advise that you aim to save 12 or 13 per cent, as you will need these extra funds to cover additional costs like stamp duty, solicitor's fees, and so on. More on that in Chapter 12.

CREDIT REPORT

The first thing you need to do is check your credit report. Go to centralcreditregister.ie and apply for your credit report. This is free, and is usually posted out within a few days. This is important because it will show up any issues with your credit history. Depending on the issue, this could take a little while to get sorted, which is why I recommend doing it as early as you can.

Here's an example of how you might encounter unexpected difficulties. I took out a five-year loan of €10,000 from a credit union to pay for my postgraduate studies to become a teacher. I never missed a payment on this loan, however I had to stop working for three six-week blocks to do my teaching practice. Credit unions are usually great to deal with, so I gave them a call and adjusted my repayments to interest only for a while to bring my repayments down while I wasn't earning any money. Being able to do this straight away over the phone was handy at the time but, in hindsight, this was a big mistake as I had no paper trail to explain the break in repayments. Between the time I took out the loan and the time I paid it back, my credit union had closed down and all accounts had been moved to another branch. Can you see where I'm going with this?

When we applied for our mortgage, a complication arose on my credit report as it showed that I had missed payments on my credit union loan, even though I had not. I had to rectify this by getting an employee in the new credit union to state in writing that the error had occurred on their end when accounts were transferred, and that I had never missed a repayment.

My credit report also showed a number of missed payments from a credit card I had when I was a student. I hadn't used this credit card in about a decade, and had never received a new card after the old one had expired, so

I cancelled the account a few months afterwards. However, the bank had tried to take fees out of that particular account and the non-payment of those fees showed up as missed payments on my credit report. Again, I had to get the bank to put in writing that they made the mistake in attempting to take fees out of a closed account.

These examples show that despite never actually missing a payment, unforeseen issues can arise, so it is important that you check your credit report as soon as you can.

CLEAN BANK STATEMENTS

We all work hard and are entitled to spend our money on whatever we wish. Once you're able to afford your lifestyle and meet all of your monthly financial commitments, then you should be free to spend the rest of your money on whatever you like. However, if you want to get a mortgage from a lender, then there are some things you just should not do:

Gambling is a red flag to underwriters (the people in the banks who decide if you'll get a mortgage or not). They simply do not like it as they believe if you're willing to gamble with your own money, you will be more than happy to gamble with theirs. Personally, it's something I have never gotten into (that and smoking, thankfully) but if it is your way of enjoying yourself then do it with cash in-person and not online or with your bank card. I would recommend closing your online betting accounts entirely.

Missing payments. If you have a loan, do not miss a payment. As in my example above, this will follow you around for years. Even missing payments on things like Netflix show up on your account as bounced payments and can show the lender that you are disorganised and not managing your money well.

Overdrafts. Lenders don't like to see loan applicants who are over-dependent on their overdraft facility. Try and avoid using it as much as you can. If you find yourself always relying on your overdraft, come up with a plan to save enough to pay it off, then cancel it. If you don't have it, you won't keep falling into it.

SAVINGS AND MORTGAGE EXEMPTIONS

You will need to show, at the very least, six months of

savings and at least two years of accounts if self-employed. Getting a deposit for a home is often the most difficult part, but hopefully you've been saving for a long time by now. Lenders love to see regular savings; the same amount, same dates ... be reliable and consistent.

Here are some tips for setting up your savings accounts so that you have money to handle the day-to-day stuff, and money being saved regularly to show you are organised and responsible with your funds.

⌇ Top tips

Set up two separate savings accounts: instant and long-term.

Use the instant savings account for bills, weddings, gifts, car insurance, unexpected bills, TV licence, etc. Think of this as your day-to-day account.

Use the long-term savings account for your deposit, rent or mortgage. Think of this as your 'how to buy a home' account.

For your instant savings account, add up all your monthly bills for the year plus extras (TV licence, holidays, car insurance, back-to-school costs, bins, etc) and divide it by whatever number of paydays you have each year (52 if paid weekly, 26 if fortnightly, 12 if monthly). You might need to estimate a few of these, so always estimate your costs to be more than expected.

Example:

- Internet: €50 per month = €600
- Phone: €35 per month = €420
- Two weddings this year: €1,000
- One holiday: €2,000
- Health insurance: €70 per month = €840
- Car insurance: €500
- TV licence: €160
- Refuse and recycling: €30 per month = €360
- Subscriptions and gym: €100 per month = €1,200

Total: €7,080

Divide this by number of paydays (monthly in this case): €7,080/12 = €590

You will likely have more expenses than this, but you get the idea. This figure is the minimum amount you should lodge into your instant savings account each payday. You should aim to put the rest into your long-term savings account.

For your long-term savings account, try to save a little bit more than your estimated mortgage repayments/rent will be (more on this in the exemption section).

Set up your savings to go out of your current account automatically on payday.

Avoid, if possible, withdrawing from your long-term savings account, especially within six months of applying for a mortgage.

🏠 Good news story

I was living away for seven years and moved home after my relationship broke down. I didn't think I had a hope of buying alone, let alone in Dublin. I found the CHP [Crazy House Prices] page and started setting up my savings according to the tips about stress testing. I also had an amazing mortgage advisor in Bank of Ireland who managed to get me an exception and I bought a one bed in Dublin 6! It's small, but it's mine, and it's so nice to have my own space.

Jenn, Dublin

MORTGAGES AND MORTGAGE EXEMPTIONS

The mortgage lending rules have recently changed. Depending on your buying status, you will need varying deposit amounts. If you're a first-time buyer (FTB) or second-/subsequent-time buyer (STB) you will need 10 per cent. If you're looking for a buy-to-let mortgage, you may need 30 per cent. If you've owned a home anywhere in the world before, you're classed as a second-time buyer (STB). This will mainly impact you if you are looking to avail of one of the government's schemes like Help to Buy (see Chapter 7).

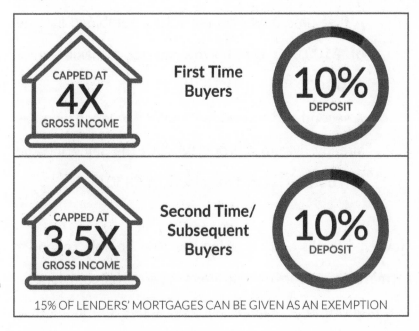

CAPPED AT **4X** GROSS INCOME

First Time Buyers — **10%** DEPOSIT

CAPPED AT **3.5X** GROSS INCOME

Second Time/ Subsequent Buyers — **10%** DEPOSIT

15% OF LENDERS' MORTGAGES CAN BE GIVEN AS AN EXEMPTION

Due to the changes in lending guidelines, the following rules now apply:

- For owner-occupiers (people who plan to live in the property they are buying), a 10 per cent deposit is typically required.

- For buy-to-let buyers (BTL – people who plan to purchase a property as an investment and rent it out), a 30 per cent deposit is typically required.

- There are also new loan-to-income limits in place, which determine how much a borrower can borrow based on their income. Here are some examples:
  - ◊ A first-time buyer couple with a combined income of €100,000 can borrow up to a maximum of €400,000.
  - ◊ A second and subsequent buyer (someone who has already owned a property) with the same income can borrow up to a maximum of €350,000.

However, banks and other lenders may be able to lend a certain amount above these limits in certain circumstances. The proportion of lending allowed above the limits may vary depending on the borrower type. It's important to note that these guidelines are not set in stone and may change over time. It's always a good idea to speak with a mortgage lender, broker or financial advisor to get a better understanding of the mortgage options available to you and the requirements you will need to meet.

Exemptions that lenders are allowed to make:

- 15 per cent of FTB lending can take place above the limits.
- 15 per cent of STB lending can take place above the limits.
- 10 per cent of BTL lending can take place above the limits.

⌐ Top tip

If you are hoping to purchase a one-bedroom property or studio, it is possible that a mortgage lender may require a higher deposit. This requirement may range from 20 to 30 per cent. This is because these types of properties have been known to depreciate in value more quickly than other types of properties. As a result, lenders may be more cautious about lending a high proportion of the purchase price on these types of properties. It is important to consider this potential requirement when searching for a home and budgeting for the purchase.

Mortgages are usually given as a maximum of 3.5 times your gross annual income (4 times if you're an FTB). This is not a given, sometimes you may be offered less. Your offer will depend on a number of factors, which I will explain below.

Now, you might look at those restrictions and requirements and think, 'Ciarán, have you seen these crazy house prices? 3.5 times my salary is not enough.' Some lenders offer what are called exemptions or exceptions (these mean the same thing) which allow you to borrow more than the typical salary cap. There are two types of exemptions:

Loan-to-income limit (LTI)

The Central Bank's rules limit the maximum amount someone can borrow (4x gross income for an FTB, 3.5x gross income for an STB) regardless of how much they earn.

So, let's say, for example, you're an FTB that earns €50,000 a year. This means you're allowed to borrow a maximum of €200,000 under the Central Bank's rules. If you're buying with a partner who also earns €50,000, that amount doubles to €400,000.

However, in any one calendar year, 15 per cent of mortgages that lenders give out to FTBs and STBs can be above this cap. In these cases, often called 'exemptions' or 'exceptions', up to 4.75 times an applicant's gross income can be lent out.

Loan-to-value ratio (LTV)

This refers to the percentage of the property's value that you can borrow and how much of it you must pay for upfront in the form of a deposit. It's often simply called 'the deposit rule'.

FTBs and STBs are required to have a 10 per cent deposit, meaning the maximum loan that can be given is 90 per cent. However, lenders are allowed to exceed this 90 per cent limit in up to 5 per cent of cases.

As an aside, I have never heard personally of a first-time buyer getting an exemption to provide less than a 10 per cent deposit. According to my research, in 2018 only 21 mortgage exemptions on LTV were given to FTBs.

Not everyone can get an exemption. And if you do, you can usually only get an exemption under one of the lending rules, not both. The vast majority of exemptions given are under the LTI rule. Some lenders grant exemptions all year round, others use up their quota of exemptions from the start of the year. Some lenders do not offer any exemptions. So, it will depend on the lender and the timing of your application.

You will need to score high on the following criteria:
- Repayment capacity
- Net disposable income
- Credit history
- Employment history
- Current account maintenance.

REPAYMENT CAPACITY

This is to show you can afford your repayments if interest rates go up. Lenders, when analysing your application, will use a stress test to gauge your ability to make repayments. For a while, lenders have been using 2 per cent above the current, available interest rate, or around 1.3 times what the repayments would be. However, with interest rates currently on the rise, these stress tests may be changing. As I outline at the beginning of this book, I am not a qualified financial advisor and recommend that you talk to one, or a broker, to be sure what the parameters are at the exact time of your application.

NET DISPOSABLE INCOME

This is the amount you have left over after paying your mortgage and all other commitments. Loans, credit cards, overdrafts and childcare costs can all impact this. The number of children you have also impacts your net disposable income. Some financial advisors would recommend that if you have a loan, do your best to pay it off before applying for a mortgage as it may impact how much a lender will allow you. However, this is case specific so make sure to get advice before using a lump sum to pay off a loan.

Lenders usually won't want to see you spending more than 40 to 50 per cent of your net income on your debts.

CREDIT HISTORY

Aim to have a clean credit history for at least five years. Any small imperfection can go against you when looking for mortgage approval. Make sure to apply for your free credit report at www.centralcreditregister.ie (see above).

EMPLOYMENT HISTORY

Ideally, you would be in the same job for at least one year before making a mortgage application. Most lenders will require you to be out of any probation period. If self-employed, you'll need at least two years' accounts. If you are in a probation period, it might be worth asking your employer if they would consider waiving this and making you permanent, as you would like to apply for a mortgage.

CURRENT ACCOUNT MAINTENANCE

You need to show that you're organised with your money. As discussed above, make sure you're not missing any payments or going into your overdraft regularly, and don't gamble.

This doesn't mean you can't spend your money as you wish; go ahead and enjoy yourself. The point is to show that you can afford the repayments, at the higher, stress test amount, alongside your regular lifestyle.

How I beat the stress test and got a 4.5x exemption

- Step 1 Go to www.ccpc.ie and figure out what your repayments will be on your mortgage. Choose whatever seems to be the average interest rate.

- Step 2 Take your monthly repayment amount and multiply it by 1.3. If your mortgage repayments are going to be €1,250 per month, you need to save (this can include rent payments) €1,250 x 1.3 = €1,625.

- Step 3 Aim to save this stress test amount every month for at least six months prior to your mortgage application. We saved it for 12 months consistently.

- This amount can include your rent and savings. So, if your rent was €1,000 per month, you need to save €625 on top of that.
- The stress test can often change, and with interest rates going up, you might do well to change this to 1.4 times your expected mortgage amount. Again, a mortgage broker or financial advisor will be better placed to help you with this.

Things to note

To get an exemption, lenders will usually want to make sure you have a property in mind. They may even require you to be sale-agreed before letting you know if you can have an exemption. Sounds counter-intuitive, but they're the rules. Banks and other lenders may consider granting exemptions to mortgage lending guidelines, such as loan-to-income limits, for borrowers with higher-than-average salaries. This is because borrowers with higher salaries are likely to have an easier time making their mortgage repayments, as they have a larger income to draw from. As a result, lenders may view these borrowers as less risky and be more willing to grant exemptions to the guidelines. It's important to note that each lender has its own policies and criteria for granting exemptions, and not all borrowers with higher salaries will necessarily be eligible. It's always a good idea to speak with a mortgage lender or financial advisor to get a better understanding of the options available to you and the requirements you will need to meet.

The mortgage lending rules are in place due to the madness with lending before the 2008 crash. In my opinion, without them, house prices would be even higher.

The 2008 financial crisis in Ireland was a period of economic downturn that was caused by the global financial crisis. During this time, the Irish economy, which relied heavily on the construction and real estate sectors, experienced a significant contraction. Many Irish banks and financial institutions struggled financially and required government bailouts. The crisis also led to high levels of unemployment and an increase in the national debt. In response, the Irish government took steps such as implementing austerity measures and structural reforms to help the country recover. It's worth noting that prior to the crisis, banks in Ireland had very few lending limits for mortgages, which contributed to the overheated housing market and ultimately to the financial crisis. The Irish economy has since recovered, but the crisis had long-term impacts on the country.

There are generally more exemptions available at the beginning of the year. I recommend using a mortgage broker, as they are clued into the market, will know which lender will suit your application best and which lenders have exemptions available.

🏠 Good news story

Became parents at 16 years old. Worked our backs off to save while renting privately with no assistance. We had years of refusals and doors closed on us. We couldn't even get the Rebuilding Ireland Home Loan, but were successful through the normal bank mortgage process eventually. Fast forward to 2021, now in our late twenties, in the midst of a pandemic, three kids and finally bought a home for our family. Never give up.

Louise, Dublin

Save regularly but live a little

This may sound a bit gloomy and you might now be thinking: 'Oh great, the fun stops here.' From personal experience, yes, you need to take great care about where your money is going (and how much of it) but this concern does not need to be all-consuming. Small changes can make a big difference and there is room to allow for some of the little luxuries you enjoy. For example, we tried to make coffees at home during the week and then go out for takeaway ones at the weekend; they tasted twice as nice. We limited takeaway food to special occasions. We always did a big grocery shop at the weekend, made something nice for dinner and bought a few nice treats. This removed the temptation to spend on takeaways every weekend and also meant we had enough food in the house to last the week. These were never steadfast rules, but in time they became pretty routine. In a strange way this discipline also encouraged more appreciation for life's simple pleasures.

Item	Coffee shop/ takeaway	Homemade	Savings per week	Savings per six months
1–2 coffees/ day @ €3/ coffee	€21–€42/ week	€5–€10	€16–€32	€416–€832
1–2 meals/day @ €10/meal	€70–€140/ week	€10–€20	€60–€120	€1,560– €3,120

As you can see, making coffee and meals at home can result in significant savings compared to buying these items from coffee shops and takeaway restaurants. For example, if you were to buy one or two coffees from a coffee shop every day, you could save up to €32 per week or €832 over a six-month period by making your coffees at home instead. These savings could potentially be used to increase the amount you are able to borrow when applying for a mortgage. It's important to keep in mind that these estimates are based on rough approximations and your actual savings may vary. It's always a good idea to carefully budget and track your expenses to get a better understanding of your financial situation and identify areas where you can save.

There's no right or wrong way to either manage or limit your spending. A friend of mine shared how every payday she would transfer a particular amount of money to her Revolut card and this would be 'fun money' for the month. Money to spend on coffees, nights out, clothes, and so on. Some months would be quieter than others, allowing funds to build, however she always stuck to what was available on the card. I'm sure you all have your own tips and tricks and will hear many more from other sources. Try a few, see what works and stick with those. Try not to let the saving become all-consuming, to the point of feeling like you need to micromanage every last cent.

🏠 Good news story

At 32, I had been two years in my job after going back to college to retrain. My wages were comparatively low compared to private sector which made buying a challenge for a single FTB. I was living with my parents and managed to save €20,000 by doing every extra shift I could. I got an exemption to get a mortgage for just €180,000. It seemed impossible to be able to buy a house in Dublin for €200,000. However, I ended up sale-agreed on a two-bed, fixer-upper in Dublin 8 for €200,000. I took out a bridging loan to do up the house, and then remortgaged to pay the loan off as my wages had gone up in the 18 months since initial mortgage application. As a public sector, single FTB, you really need to be creative to make it in Dublin!

Ciara, Dublin

ACTION STEPS

- Get your credit report.
- Decide if you are going to use a broker or go directly to lenders.
- Get your filing cabinet.
- Get your savings plan in place.
- Get your bank accounts clean and organised.

3
APPLYING FOR A MORTGAGE

THIS chapter will guide you on how to gather all necessary documents and information. This includes personal identification documents, financial documents, and any other documents required by lenders or brokers.

- Research lenders and brokers. Compare different options, consider factors such as reputation and customer service, and make a list of potential lenders and brokers to contact.

- Understand the mortgage approval process. This includes knowing the difference between an 'approval in principle' (AIP) and a full mortgage approval, and being aware of the documents and information required for each.

- Plan your home search. Determine your budget and target price range, consider the location, size, and type of property you are looking for, and make a list of potential properties to visit.

- Prepare for potential delays or challenges. Be patient as the mortgage application process can take longer than expected, and be prepared for potential hold-ups or setbacks. Consider seeking professional advice or assistance if needed.

This chapter will give you all of the information and documents that are needed to apply for your mortgage. There will be times during this process when you will get angry, and parts of the process are excruciatingly slow. This is a common theme when it comes to buying a home in Ireland ... everything seems very slow. Which is why Chapter 1 is so important: the more organised you are, the less hold-ups there will be in your application.

My wife and I have gone through this process twice now; once for buying our house and then again when we switched our mortgage provider. When we switched mortgage provider, it still took nearly two months to draw down the money, and that is despite it being a far simpler task than buying a new home. So, you're going to have to be patient. This sluggishness is down to a combination of huge numbers of applications and a lack of staff within the lenders. We have also seen a number of lenders choose to leave the mortgage market here, which has added to the problems.

APPROVAL IN PRINCIPLE (AIP)

Before you start looking at properties, start applying to lenders to try to get 'approval in principle'. This means you have been given the go-ahead from a lender to go 'home shopping'. It indicates that you will get mortgage approval, and will also provide you with an idea of the amount you can borrow. It is also an advantage to have this when it comes to making an offer on a property as sellers are more likely to accept an offer if they know you have mortgage approval. I would advise that everyone do this; it can be frustrating for all involved if people are bidding on homes without having AIP, as the price can be driven up even though certain bidders are not in a position to buy. Most estate agents will ask for evidence of your AIP before they allow you to put an offer in.

Mortgage AIP is not the same for all lenders; some have their AIP 'underwritten'. This means that they have gone through your accounts and you are more likely to get approval for the amount listed. Some lenders do not underwrite their AIP. Estate agents will know which AIPs are underwritten, and which are not. If yours is underwritten, it puts you in a stronger position when bidding on a home.

There are two main types of mortgage approval: underwritten and non-underwritten.

With underwritten mortgage approval, a mortgage underwriter takes a closer look at your financial situation. They'll review your credit history, job history, income, debts, and other financial factors to see if you meet the lender's guidelines for a mortgage.

Non-underwritten mortgage approval is a bit different. The lender might use pre-approved guidelines or automated underwriting systems to decide if you meet their requirements for a mortgage loan. Sometimes non-underwritten mortgage approval is based on a calculation of your gross income, which isn't as detailed as a more in-depth credit check and may not fully assess your creditworthiness.

It's important to know that underwritten mortgage approval is generally considered more reliable and secure than non-underwritten mortgage approval. This is because the underwritten approval process is more thorough and less likely to result in mistakes that could impact your ability to get a mortgage.

If you want to make sure your mortgage approval is underwritten to avoid any unnecessary delays after going sale-agreed, you could ask your lender about it. It's always a good idea to communicate with your lender and make sure you understand the process and any potential risks or issues that may arise. This can help you feel more confident and prepared as you move forward on your home-buying journey.

Do I need to show my AIP to the estate agent?

Yes, usually you do, but I would advise that you redact the amount you are approved for. A lot of estate agents will insist on seeing the amount. In this case, you could ask your lender or solicitor to write an email or letter to say that you have the funds to back up your offer. I do not think it's a good idea to show an estate agent how much money you have to spend. It equates to playing a game of poker with your cards on show.

Imagine this scenario: you have approval for €350,000 plus your €35,000 deposit (€385,000 in total). You're bidding on a home that is priced at €300,000. If you show your AIP to the agent, they know you have another €85,000 to spend.

Estate agents will use every trick in the book to get you to increase your offer. At the end of the day, they work for the vendor and it's their job to get the vendor, not you, the best deal.

Make sure to use a mortgage rate comparison site to understand what your monthly repayments will be. The CCPC one is fantastic and impartial.

Borrowing to your maximum capacity

As I've already discussed, most people can borrow up to 3.5x their gross income. First-time buyers can borrow up to 4 times their gross income and if you can manage to get an exemption, you could potentially borrow up to 4.75

times your gross income. Is this a good idea though?

There are a few potential issues with borrowing to your maximum capacity for a mortgage. One of the main concerns is affordability: if you borrow the maximum amount you can, you might have a hard time paying your monthly mortgage payments, especially if something unexpected happens or your financial situation changes. Plus, if interest rates go up, your payments will increase. High levels of debt can also be a financial burden and make it hard to pay off other debts or save for the future, as well as being a huge mental stress. If you borrow to your max, you might not have much financial flexibility to make other big purchases or handle unexpected expenses. Finally, there's the risk of defaulting on your mortgage if you can't make your payments, which could result in losing your home and damaging your ability to access loans or credit in the future.

It is important to consider the potential changes to your financial situation when deciding on a mortgage. These changes could include the loss of a job, the addition of childcare expenses, or the need for one person to stop working. It is crucial to ensure that you will be able to afford your mortgage repayments in the event of these changes. This will help to avoid financial difficulties and the risk of defaulting on your mortgage.

On the other hand, it's worth considering that rents are currently at an all-time high. Even if you borrow to your maximum capacity for a mortgage, your monthly payments might still be lower than your monthly rent. That's something to keep in mind as you weigh the pros and cons of borrowing to your max. It's always a good idea to carefully consider your financial situation and capabilities before deciding how much to borrow for a mortgage. It might be more financially secure to borrow a smaller amount and have a lower monthly mortgage payment, even if it means saving longer to afford a larger deposit.

LENDERS AND ADVISORS

You can apply for a mortgage by:

1. Applying directly to a lender such as a bank or credit union or local authority and dealing with them and looking after the application process yourself, or

2. Using a mortgage broker to deal with lenders on your behalf and advise you during the process. At the beginning it is important to ask the broker for their terms of business, what they charge and how many lenders they represent. Most brokers are free, and get their fee from the lender.

⌐ Top tip

Personally, I found using a broker to be excellent as they knew the market and the best lender for us to apply to. I know other buyers who have had great success going it alone. So, it's up to you. A mortgage broker might only apply to one lender on your behalf – the lender they feel will best match your requirements. Brokers may charge a fee if they go through the approval process for you but you then decide not to continue on your home-buying journey. This fee is to cover the costs of the time they invested in your application.

Documents you may need

You will need certain documents when you apply for a mortgage and you should keep a copy of anything you give to a lender or broker.

- Proof of identification, proof of address and proof of your personal public service number (PPSN)
- Proof of income: latest P60, payslips, certified accounts if self-employed
- Evidence of how you manage your money. This will require your current and loan account statements for the last three to twelve months (including Revolut), depending on the lender.

When applying

If going alone, apply to more than one lender and compare their rates and offers carefully, rather than panicking and accepting the first offer.

Don't be swayed by introductory offers such as cash back. These can be rewarding in the short-term but that particular mortgage could end up costing you more over the life of the loan if it has a higher interest rate. Make sure to crunch the numbers and do your research to compare the lifetime costs and benefits of different offers. There's an app called Karl's Mortgage Calculator that can do this for you. I don't know who Karl is, but his app is handy and is also available at drcalculator.com/mortgage.

Here is an example of a €300,000 mortgage over 30 years:

Mortgage	Interest rate	Term (years)	Cashback	Monthly payment	Total interest	Total paid
1	3.5%	30	0%	€1,347	€184,968	€484,968
2	4.2%	30	2%	€1,467	€228,138	€528,138

In example 2, you will get €6,000 cashback after you draw down your mortgage (2 per cent of €300,000). However, over the length of the mortgage you are paying nearly €43,000 more in interest. This is not a perfect example as it implies the mortgage is fixed at those rates over the 30 years, but it's a good way to visualise how much extra some cashback offers actually cost you.

It's important to consider both the interest rate and the cashback when choosing a mortgage, as they can have a significant impact on the overall cost of the loan. You should carefully evaluate your financial situation and consider your long-term goals when deciding on a mortgage.

What do lenders base their decision on?

- Income. Lenders will look at your annual income and may take bonuses and overtime into account. They may factor in rental income if you plan to rent out a room, although this is rare since the 2008 financial crash.

- Your age may be a factor. Lenders have an upper age limit they require a loan to be paid off by, typically between 65 and 70. So if you are over 40 years of age and seeking a mortgage with a term of 30 years you may have difficulty getting approval.

- Outstanding loans or a high credit card balance may reduce the amount you can borrow or may affect your ability to get a mortgage.

- Employment status. A lender will look at whether you are in permanent employment or on probation. If you work on contract they may require you to be employed for at least 22 months with the same employer or be on a second contract with the same employer.

- Residential status. Are you a resident in Ireland or a returning emigrant?

- Outgoings. Lenders will take your other financial commitments, such as childcare, into consideration.

- Money management. Lenders will look at your bank statements and assess your ability to meet direct debits and standing orders. They will take note if you are using an overdraft facility on a regular basis and if there is evidence of excessive online gambling.

- Savings prove that you have put aside enough for your deposit and have the ability to save a set amount of money on a regular basis.

- Credit history shows your track record of paying loans in the past. A poor credit history can prevent you from getting a mortgage.

- Property value. Lenders like to know the purchase price of the home you want to buy (if you have one in mind) and the value of your current home, if you plan to sell and buy a new home.

- Amount you wish to borrow. This is the amount you are applying to borrow and is the difference between the purchase price of the property and the deposit you have saved.

- Number of applicants. Are you borrowing by yourself or with someone else?

- Type of purchase. In general, it's advisable that first-time buyers avoid buying a home at auction as these sales are 'sold as seen'. If there are any structural issues, you're on your own and legally obliged to follow through with the purchase. Most lenders would view this type of purchase as high risk.

SELF-EMPLOYED

If you are self-employed, the information you will need to supply varies depending on the mortgage lender you choose, but it usually includes the following.

- Your financial accounts. These will need to be certified by an accountant and most lenders ask for at least two years of accounts.

- Your bank statements. Provide your current accounts, credit cards and business accounts for at least the previous six months.

- Your Revenue documents. This normally consists of your Revenue certificates, and your tax clearance certificate for the last two years.

- Other business information. If you have copies of larger business contracts or forthcoming contracts, you may be able to submit these as evidence to support your application.

- Lenders will work off the average of tax returns for the preceding two years. If your income was €30,000 one year and €40,000 the next, they will work off €35,000.

🏠 **Good news story**

I am a first-time buyer doing it on my own as a one-person buyer. I moved back to Ireland from living abroad for four years in the middle of Covid, end of 2020. I had a decent amount of savings and was probably a bit naive, thinking I would be sorted with a new house in six months or so. Two years later, I am now sale-agreed and in the final stages of contracts, etc. It has been a process, being outbid, mad seller expectations of what their house is worth, delays

---

> with banks being slow to process things and the rest!
> But I can see the light at the end of the tunnel. I am
> hoping to get my keys in the next few weeks to be in
> before Christmas. My own house in the area I wanted
> to buy in. Best Christmas present!
> *Stephen, Dublin*

ONE STEP FORWARD, TWO BACK

This process may feel like walking a tightrope. There also may be plenty of falls which leave you back at what feels like the starting point again. We found ourselves continuously checking emails hoping for progression, but instead were often disappointed that there had been another hold-up or setback. It is worth remembering that mortgage providers make a lot of money off you. Depending on the interest rate and the term of the loan, they could be earning €2 back for every €1 they lend to you. This was something that frustrated me throughout the process; I often felt like the bank were treating me as if they were giving me the loan for free and doing me a favour.

Here is an example of just how much money a bank

makes from a mortgage of €405,000 at 5 per cent over 35 years.

Property	€450,000
Deposit	€45,000
Principal	€405,000
Interest	5%
Term	35 years
Payment	€2,043.99
Start date	1 October 2023
End date	1 September 2058
Length	35 years
Total interest	€453,473.73
Total payment	€858,473.73

Note especially how much interest you pay. You borrow €405,000 but repay the bank €858,473.73. That means the bank is making €453,473.73 in profit from you. So, if you don't succeed with one lender, take your money elsewhere! Again, much of the language used and the documentation we were required to produce were foreign to us until we embarked on this process. Which is why, again, I cannot stress enough the importance of familiarising yourself with what is needed and having everything organised before starting out. You're already a step ahead having bought this book and read this far!

FIXED RATE OR VARIABLE RATE

A fixed-rate mortgage is a type of mortgage where the interest rate stays the same for a certain period of time, usually a few years. This can have the following pros:

- Predictable monthly payments. You will know exactly what your monthly mortgage payment will be for the entire fixed-rate term, making budgeting and financial planning easier.

- Protection against rising interest rates. If interest rates rise during the term of the loan, your monthly mortgage payments will not be affected.

However, fixed-rate mortgages also have the following drawback:

- Limited flexibility. With a fixed-rate mortgage, if you want to switch to a different mortgage provider, you may incur a 'breakout fee' which means you will have to pay a sum of money to get out of the contract.

A variable-rate mortgage is a type of mortgage where the interest rate can fluctuate based on changes in market interest rates. This type of mortgage can have the following benefit:

- Potential for lower monthly payments. If interest rates decline during the term of the loan, your monthly mortgage payments may also decline, providing some financial relief.

However, variable-rate mortgages also have the following drawback:

- Risk of rising interest rates. If interest rates rise during the term of the loan, your monthly mortgage payments may also increase, which could be a financial burden if you are not prepared for higher payments.

Generally, it is advisable to opt for a fixed-term rate, especially during times of rising interest rates.

⊶ Top tip

If you are looking to buy a home on land that is more than one acre, you may need to show the lender that you won't use it for commercial purposes. There may be a higher stamp duty for the remaining land over one acre and public liability insurance. If you're looking at a home on more than an acre, it is best to seek advice from your lender.

🏠 Good news story

In February 2022, myself and my partner were due to build: had the site, drawings, guide quote, en route to completing the planning application. My gut feeling was to ask for an up-to-date quote due to the extortionate and unpredictable rising costs for building. I got a revised bill: a 128m² bungalow (for a turnkey finish) went from €238,000 to over €280,000 in less than five months.

I started crying. Consulted himself and asked him to choose the life he wanted to live. Either years and years with a tight budget or to look at houses for sale.

I was like a dog with a bone – every house online checked that night. Emailed an estate agent around 10 p.m. Estate agent replied at 10.20 p.m., invited me to a viewing (that my fella couldn't attend).

So, I went alone. Felt absolutely like the house was for us and he trusted my gut. How lucky am I?

Started bidding on it. It was back and over for around two weeks and with our last €1,000 we submitted our last bid and won the bid (€25,000 more than the asking price!). The AIP was due to expire five days later.

We are in the house since July 2022 and absolutely thrilled. Everything has worked out. We still have the site and hopefully things will settle in years to come and we get the chance to build. Worst case, we will have something for our children to get them started.

Stephanie, Galway

ACTION STEPS

- Use a comparison site to check out all current mortgage providers' rates.
- Get your documents in order and ready to send.
- If self-employed, make sure your accounts and Revenue documents are organised.

4

RENOVATION AND SELF-BUILD MORTGAGES

BRIEF overview of this chapter:

- Gather detailed information about your current financial situation, including credit report, employment status, and income.

- Create a detailed renovation plan that includes the scope of work, cost estimates, and timeline for completion.

- Obtain quotes from contractors or other professionals for any work that will be done as part of the renovation.

- Gather documentation of the property and any plans or drawings.

- Consider hiring an engineer or quantity surveyor to help with cost estimates for the renovation. This may be required by the lender as part of the mortgage application process.

Renovation mortgages deserve their own chapter because they are an underutilised option and should be more common. There are a few reasons for this but the main one is: renovation mortgages are very difficult to get. A renovation mortgage is basically when the bank gives you money to buy a home that needs renovating, and then gives you the money to renovate it. Sounds too good to be true? Not quite.

I am a huge fan of RTÉ's *Room to Improve*. I love watching people build their dream homes and it's always something I wanted to do myself. Buying an old house and fixing it up was always our preference (partly because new-builds were too expensive but mostly because when you buy an older house, you are usually buying into an already well-established community and it gives you the opportunity to customise the house to suit your needs) so we had always planned on getting a renovation mortgage. Our broker told us we would qualify so we went all-in on finding a fixer-upper. Now, I am absolutely not a DIY expert but I had time and energy (this was before we had a baby) so figured I could do as much of the work as possible myself and then my friends in the trades would help with the complicated stuff. Long story short, we went sale-agreed and everything was moving along fine until we got our loan offer and it had no mention of the renovation money in it.

When I queried this with our mortgage broker, he explained that because the survey said the house was habitable, the lender was unwilling to lend us the extra €45,000 that was promised to help with the renovations. This was devastating for us (and still is) as we loved the house but it most certainly needed to be renovated. We went ahead with the purchase anyway, without the extra €45,000 and with an attitude that we would figure it out. We still had some savings so we used those funds to help with the renovation and we went to the credit union to secure the rest. As teachers, we had access to Comhar Linn Credit Union which is the credit union for primary school teachers. They are exceptionally good to deal with and we had our loan in our account the next working day.

One big problem with the credit union loan is that the rate is 6.5 per cent over ten years, whereas our mortgage was only 2.35 per cent, fixed for three years. The difference in monthly payments is huge. My point is: renovation mortgages are very difficult to get but they shouldn't be. In my opinion, the government should provide zero per cent interest loans for people to renovate and retrofit old homes. Without some sort of intervention, older homes requiring renovations and retrofitting will mostly be sold to investors as they will be the only ones with enough cash to do them up. We also have massive climate targets to hit, on a national scale, and retrofitting older homes is far more sustainable than building new ones (although we need to do both).

Here, I will outline what a renovation mortgage is in more detail. Your lender will require some accurate costings, so you might need to pay for an engineer and/or a quantity surveyor to help you with those.

RENOVATION MORTGAGES

There are two types of renovations for your home, structural and non-structural, and they are treated very differently. The big question is this: is the home habitable, does it have a working kitchen, bathroom, water, heating? If it is not habitable, then the only option is to try and get your mortgage provider to lend you the funds to do the work, as you will most likely not get a mortgage on a property that cannot be lived in with a view to doing work at a point in the future.

Non-structural renovations

Non-structural renovation mortgages are possible if you are buying a property which can be lived in or needs something minor, like a kitchen, to make it habitable. These works normally involve cosmetic elements such as a kitchen upgrade, new windows, bathroom or doors.

For this application to work, a lender must be made aware in advance of the type of work that you plan on doing and this assessment becomes part of the application. It involves a two-stage valuation process which must be carried out by the same valuer.

The first valuation will give a current value based on the purchase price and a valuation assuming the works are carried out. The second valuation occurs after the works are done to the property. The property value must increase, as a minimum, in line with what you are spending on the renovations. For example, if the purchase price is €200,000 and the works cost €30,000, the new value of the property must be above €230,000.

Now for the tricky bit. The monies for the renovation will not be released until the works are completed. This is called a hold back, which means you will have to fund any renovations up front and get the money back from the lender once works are complete and the valuer has confirmed the property value has increased in line with expectations.

This means you are back to the same issue I had: you're going to have to find the money somewhere. You could do as we did and get a credit union loan and pay it back with the money released from your lender after the works are complete (credit unions generally don't have early payment penalties). At least with this option, you only pay the higher interest rate loan for a short period and then when that is paid off, the costs will be spread over the term of your mortgage at a much lower interest rate.

To simplify that for you, your mortgage will most likely be the lowest interest rate loan you'll ever get. Loans from banks and credit unions are usually at a much higher interest rate. So, if the works cost €30,000 and the bank has agreed that they will loan this to you as part of your renovation mortgage (low interest rate), you'll have to get a loan from elsewhere to pay for the works (higher interest rate). Then, once the works are done, the bank releases that €30,000 they promised you and you can pay off the higher interest rate loan.

The other option is to find an extremely generous and accommodating builder who will agree to do all of the work pending payment at the end. Good luck finding one of those!

How much can I borrow?

If you are a first time buyer (FTB), you can borrow 90 per cent of the purchase price and up to 90 per cent of the renovation costs. If you are a second time buyer (STB), this becomes 80 per cent in both scenarios (unless this changes with the new lending rules).

Here's an example:

- Home price: €200,000
- Renovation costs: €50,000

If you are an FTB, you will need 10 per cent of each sum as a deposit. This equates to €20,000 and €5,000, a total deposit of €25,000.

An STB will need 20 per cent of each sum, a €50,000 deposit in total.

For non-structural works, I am told that lenders will only consider loans up to approximately €40,000. You should query this with your mortgage broker or advisor though. Both the additional borrowing and the initial mortgage are subject to the lender's income multiples (4x maximum based on income would need to cover both loans or you may get an exemption/exception if available).

In the case of the example above, your household income, as an FTB, would need to be at least €63,000 to qualify: €63,000 x 4 = €252,000 (unless you can get an exemption).

Structural renovations

A structural renovation means something is being removed

from or added to the property, such as an extension. It is very different to a non-structural renovation as you must employ the services of an architect or engineer to oversee all works and approve the costings.

This has to be applied for when you are doing the initial mortgage application. Ideally, planning permission should already be in place, or as a minimum the lender needs to be made aware that you will be applying for planning permission and starting works within six months of the initial mortgage drawdown.

There is a two-stage valuation process which must be carried out by the same valuer. The first valuation will give a current value based on the purchase price and a valuation assuming the works are carried out; the second valuation confirms the works have been done and completed.

With this type of work, a lender would expect there to be an uplift in the value of the property and most look for at least 20 per cent equity being in the property once the works are complete. Equity in a home is the portion of the property that is owned outright by you, the borrower, as opposed to the portion that is being financed through a mortgage. So, in this example, the bank will want you to have at least 20 per cent equity in the home.

The money to cover the works are again held back until after the works are done, however for large renovations the money is released in stages once your engineer signs off on the work completed at each stage. For example, the laying of foundations could be classed as stage one, the building of walls and the roof as stage two, and so on. You would need to fund each stage in advance, or ask your builder to wait for monies to be released by the lender.

How much can I borrow?

As above, if you are an FTB, you can borrow 90 per cent of the purchase price and up to 90 per cent of the renovation subject to an uplift in the valuation that will leave at least 20 per cent equity in the property.

Here's another example:

- Home price: €100,000

- Renovation costs: €100,000

As an FTB, you will need 10 per cent of each sum as a deposit, totalling €20,000 (€10,000 and €10,000).

You borrow €90,000 for the home and €90,000 for the renovations. Total borrowing = €180,000.

The value of the home after the works needs to be a minimum of €225,000, so that you have at least 20 per cent equity in the home. 80 per cent of €225,000 = €180,000, which is what the bank has loaned out to you.

In the past, an STB would need 20 per cent of each sum, totalling €40,000 (€20,000 and €20,000). Again, the amount of the mortgage must fall under the 3.5x lending limit unless you get an exemption. However, this may now be changed to 10 per cent with the new lending rules as of January 1st 2023.

As you can see from the above examples, even if you do manage to get a renovation mortgage, it is not a straightforward process and you will need to be able to fund the works yourself in advance. This is why I firmly believe the government should step in to help by providing zero per cent or low interest loans to help owner-occupiers. We have over 180,000 vacant and derelict properties in Ireland and we are in the middle of both a housing and climate crisis. Renovating and retrofitting older homes is part of the solution to both. It is far more environmentally friendly to renovate existing homes that already have services and foundations in place than building all new homes from scratch.

Self-build mortgages

Self-build mortgages are for people who want to build their own home. These are a lot more common than renovation mortgages and are an especially good option if people are gifted land or a site. There are issues in Ireland with attaining planning permission, but those issues vary from county to county and are beyond the scope of this book.

There are a number of stages to work through in building your own home: buying or acquiring a site, getting planning permission for the build, and finally building your home. This can take a lot longer than buying a house, but the benefit is that you are getting a custom-built home just for you and your needs.

First-time buyers and second-time buyers

You'll need at least a 10 per cent deposit. The maximum

loan to value (LTV) is 90 per cent of the site cost or value plus the cost of construction, or 90 per cent of the valuation on completion – whichever is lower.

Your site can be your deposit. If a site is gifted to you or already owned by you, you are in a position to borrow 100 per cent of the build costs. However, you may also need at least 10 per cent of the total cost as a contingency for any unforeseen costs.

Planning

You can apply for a self-build mortgage before you have planning permission; however, each lender deals with these differently so it will depend on the lender you use as some will require planning permission to be in place.

There are two ways you can go about your build: direct labour or fixed contract.

Direct labour

In this scenario, you are in complete control, which, depending on your prior experiences, may be good or bad. You will have to oversee worker contracts for all phases of the build, from the foundation to the finishing touches, under the guidance of your chosen architect. Do you know how to organise your plastering, roofing, drainage and sewage? If you think that this would be a difficult undertaking, you might decide to hire a professional builder to complete the build on your behalf. Managing a self-build is a difficult task that needs a lot of time and effort. It will basically feel like a full-time job.

Fixed contract

If the direct labour approach seems like too much to handle, then using a builder or construction company might be a better idea. The entire build will be managed by the builder under the direction of your architect. A lot of architects have good relationships with builders, so they may be able to recommend someone they know and trust and have worked well with in the past. It may also be advisable to hire a project manager and/or quantity surveyor. I have watched enough *Room to Improve* to know that if it was me, I would definitely be hiring the professionals.

Stages involved

Stage payments occur when the lender releases money to cover a specific part of the build. The number of stages differs depending on your individual circumstances. For example, if you have already bought a site, you will skip the first stage. There are usually between four and six payment stages. They can include:

- Buying the site
- Preparing the site and foundations
- Building the floor level
- Building the roof level, i.e. the property's frame or shell
- Finishing the property, i.e. electrical wiring and plumbing, making it liveable
- Receiving the certificate of compliance and having the final valuation done.

Each stage of the build must be certified by an official certifier before payment can be released. Payments are requested each time via your solicitor. You will also need self-build insurance which may also be referred to as home under construction insurance. We actually got this for our renovations, as the house was vacant during the building works period and so would not fall under the terms of standard home insurance. It was pretty cheap, only around €250 for the year.

Self-builds also fall under the Help to Buy scheme, which I talk about in Chapter 7.

Just a note of caution on self-builds. They are not for the faint-hearted and I would guess that it would be nearly impossible for someone working a full-time job to be able to project manage it themselves. There are also a lot of costs involved, one of the biggest being council fees. I have heard these range anywhere from €2,000 to €20,000, depending on which council you're dealing with. This book is titled 'How to Buy a Home', not 'How to Build a Home' as my knowledge in this area is very limited, so I would recommend getting a lot of professional advice if you're planning on going down the self-build route.

🏠 Good news story

We got married in August 2021 and we were living

with the in-laws, trying to save for a mortgage. My sister recommended I follow your page. We bought your home-buyer's guide and went from there. We quickly realised that we wouldn't have the budget to buy a home on our salaries and decided we'd save that bit more and try to get an exemption. Things were tight but we managed.

Come January, we applied to the banks and successfully got an exemption with AIB. We began our house-hunting journey, which was soul destroying at times, but one day I received an email about houses for sale in a new development. I called the auctioneer and the houses were all gone within half an hour of receiving the email. The auctioneer stuck us on the cancellation list. Lo and behold, I got the call the next day! The auctioneer informed us that people often book multiple houses in different developments, in case they don't get where they want. When he became aware the buyer wasn't genuine, he cancelled it on them. The house wasn't finished yet but that gave us more time to plan and save.

> We are now just a few weeks away from moving in and we really can't thank you or your page enough, for all the guidance and tips for buying a home. Even reading the good news stories kept us going when times got tough and we felt like giving up.
>
> *Nicola, Dublin*

10 TIPS BEFORE BUILDING YOUR HOME

1. Choose a good architect: this could make or break your stress levels throughout the entire process. Get a recommendation from someone you know. I have heard some horror stories from friends who have used the wrong architect, and I have heard some amazing stories from people whose architect was amazing. Do your research.

2. Whenever you pay money for something, insist on a receipt. You'll need these.

3. Applying for planning permission is complicated, confusing and time-consuming. Your architect will help with this and it may be helpful if the architect has experience with self-builds in the local area. You can

check out myplan.ie and look at what planning has been granted nearby for some ideas as to what should be given approval. You should not start any works until you receive the full grant of permission.

4. Make sure all tradespeople employed are insured and have the relevant certifications.

5. Try to get at least three quotes from everyone you will be employing directly. To get an accurate quote you'll need to supply the trades with as much information about your build as possible, including:

   - A full set of accurate and current plans and drawings
   - Specification documentation
   - Details of any materials you want and any you will be providing
   - Details of any work you will be handling or subcontracting
   - Details of any preliminaries (for example, site clearance, demolition, etc)
   - Make sure each quote clearly shows the tradesperson's name, address and telephone number.

6. 'Buy cheap, buy twice!' Don't just choose the cheapest

quote. Also, it is important to remember that an estimate is not equal to a quotation. An estimate is a back-of-a-beer-mat type of figure, whereas a quotation should be a written, exact price for the job. Don't hire off the back of an estimate, always get a full quote.

7. Carefully go through all quotes and make sure that everything you've asked for is included. Don't forget about VAT, sometimes quotes will be exclusive of VAT which adds on a hefty chunk. If you're adding work on after the original quote, make sure to get an updated and revised quote. Check, too, if the work is guaranteed and if guarantees are insurance-backed. Ask to see the tradesperson's public liability insurance certificate.

8. When you are building your own home, you need to be aware of radon, a colourless, odourless and tasteless naturally occurring radioactive gas, which is prevalent in some parts of the country. You should install a radon barrier and sumps at the time of construction as this will greatly reduce the cost and the disruption associated with remediation. Once your house is built, test for radon over a minimum three-month period to assess

radon levels. The test costs from €40.

9. Make sure you insure your site and your build.

10. Don't pay the final sum until everything, including your snag list, is finished to your liking. There should be a final reinspection before the process is signed off.

🏠 Good news story

We bought an apartment near IKEA in the boom (2006) for €270,000. It was great at the time and we've great memories and friends we made there for life. But in 2015 we had our first child and felt we needed a bigger space and nicer surroundings for the future. Feeling trapped as we still owed over €180,000 on the mortgage, the most expensive recent property sale being only €140,000, having no way to save 20 per cent deposit for a new purchase, we dropped into the local Ulster Bank branch in Charlestown shopping centre and the manager was great; she said it was her mission to help us move.

After two meetings, we were on our way to

purchasing a three-bedroom semi-detached house in Donabate for €280,000. We got an exemption from the 20 per cent rule as we owned a property in negative equity. We sold the apartment for €187,510 and carried the balance to our new mortgage. We didn't need any deposit and our savings were used to modernise the property. It was honestly the best move we ever made and even though we thought it wasn't going to be possible, all it took was a couple of thirty-minute meetings with the bank to make it happen.

Cathal, Dublin

The information contained in chapters 2 and 3 of this book is quite detailed and will need some time to get to grips with. In my opinion, it would be a good idea to use a mortgage broker to hold your hand through all of this. Most brokers don't charge a fee, and get their income from the lender. Some brokers do charge a fee, which I think is only right as they put a huge amount of time into your application. If a mortgage broker does charge, the fee is usually small enough (around €300) and, in my opinion, it is some of the best money you will spend throughout the entire process. Go with a recommendation from someone you know.

The mortgage market is turbulent and changes week to week. A good mortgage broker will know:

- the current market very well
- which lender will suit your application best
- which lenders have exemptions available
- which lenders are slow and which are moving along quickly.

They can also supply lots more valuable information. We used a mortgage broker for our first mortgage, then went directly to a lender for our switch. We had fantastic experiences with both, however for the switch I was far more aware of what was needed. So, if this is your first time getting a mortgage, I recommend going to a broker for advice.

ACTION STEPS

- Engage with a mortgage broker or a qualified financial planner.
- Get recommendations and quotes from professionals (architect, builder, trades).
- Decide if you want to go down the route of direct labour or fixed contract.

5
CHOOSING A SOLICITOR

A BRIEF summary of this chapter:

- Experience: Look for a solicitor who has experience in handling conveyancing transactions. They should be familiar with the process and any potential issues that may arise.

- Reputation: It is important to choose a solicitor who has a good reputation in the industry. You can ask for references from previous clients or check online reviews to get a sense of the solicitor's reputation. I always recommend using a solicitor that has been referred by a friend or colleague.

- Communication: It is important to choose a solicitor who is responsive and keeps you informed throughout the process. Look for a solicitor who is easy to get in touch with and answers your questions promptly.

- Fees: Make sure to shop around and compare fees from

different solicitors to ensure you are getting a fair price. Be sure to ask about any hidden fees that may not be included in the initial quote.

When buying a home, you need a solicitor. The job your solicitor will do is called conveyancing. This word describes the transfer of ownership of a property and the jobs the solicitor does to help with your home purchase. Once you go sale-agreed, i.e. agree on a sale price with the vendor (vendor is the word used to describe the person who owns the property that is being sold), the first thing you will be asked for is your solicitor's details. It's wise to have one organised early on in your home-buying process.

One of the most surprising things I learned when we bought our home off-market is just how much of the whole process is done by solicitors. Once you go sale-agreed, your solicitor becomes the most important person you deal with. Our solicitor was fantastic, and generally responded to emails within hours. In my experience, from listening to people's stories, the majority of buyers have positive experiences with solicitors. However, if you wind up with one that turns out to be not-so-great, your choice can potentially result in you losing out on the home due to delays with paperwork resulting in vendors going back to the market. Make sure you choose wisely.

USE RECOMMENDATIONS

A good solicitor can make or break your home-buying journey. Make sure to get recommendations from friends or from trusted online groups or pages. It is a good idea to have a solicitor in place before you start viewing properties because you might just get lucky and go sale-agreed very quickly. If you do make an offer and it is accepted, the estate agent will ask for your solicitor's details to pass onto the vendor's solicitor.

🏠 **Good news story**

This felt like our last chance to apply for a mortgage due to age. I stayed at home with the children until they were established in school. I then went back to education to earn a degree. So, we were in the older cohort and the husband was self-employed. After bad

---

advice from one broker, we found another one who gave us the best and no-nonsense advice.

When we heard we could get a mortgage I started following Crazy House Prices on Instagram.

I made a strategy plan with all I learned from the page for when we could start bidding on houses.

My plan was to view a few houses available and this would let us see the neighbourhoods where we would write letters to if we were outbid for some houses.

In the first week of viewing, we fell in love with a house. Viewed it again and put in the asking price bid the next morning. We were blown away when the offer was accepted the very same day.

Now the contracts are signed and waiting to draw down in the next few days. Can't wait for the teens to choose the colour of their room for the first time ever in their lives. By the time the book is released we will be settled in and all.

Mandie, Dublin

SEARCHES

I had no idea what 'searches' were so I thought it would be a good idea to write about them in this book. As a buyer, there are many requirements that you would not be aware of. This is where your solicitor earns their corn. They perform a lot of checks and searches and will list these on their invoice so you know what they were. They will check that the sale of the property is legal, that the person who is selling the property owns it and has the right to sell it, and that nobody else could claim to own it.

Some searches are done before contracts are drawn up, and some are done afterwards. You don't need to know every single detail of these, that's the solicitor's job, but I will summarise them below.

Pre-contract searches

Planning search. This checks to ensure that the property is zoned as residential and whether there are any other planning issues that need to be known.

A compulsory purchase order search finds out if the property has been bought by a local authority, which would mean it cannot be sold to you. It would be very rare that a house being advertised for sale has this issue, but it needs to be checked to be sure.

Day-of-closing searches

These searches are done to ensure nothing has changed since the contracts were signed.

- A land registry search confirms the vendor actually owns the property and is legally allowed to sell it.

- A judgement search ensures the vendor has no outstanding mortgage issues, such as non-payment of debt. It will also show if any litigation is pending against the property or vendor.

- A bankruptcy search shows if the vendor has been declared bankrupt. If they have been, the property is not theirs to sell.

- A registry of deeds search is required to confirm that the title of the property is registered.

If any of these searches uncovers a potential problem, the matter can be raised with the vendor and their solicitor.

There may be a simple explanation. If not, you may not want (or you may not be able) to proceed with the transaction.

Fees

Solicitor's fees can vary considerably so it is a good idea to shop around, but remember that having a good solicitor is very important. This is, most likely, the biggest purchase of your life. Don't make your choice based on a solicitor's fee alone. They will usually break their fee down into different parts.

Fees subject to VAT

- Professional fees (plus 23 per cent VAT)
- Postage, paper (plus 23 per cent VAT)

Other outlays not subject to VAT

- Land registry fee on deed of transfer
- Land registry fee on mortgage deed
- Stamp duty (this is calculated as 1 per cent of the purchase price of your home)
- Folio and filed plan

- Search fees

🔑 Top tip

A folio is a number that identifies a specific property. A filed plan is a map that shows where the property is and its boundaries. These documents are used in the process of transferring a property from one person to another. The seller's solicitor will give copies of these documents to the buyer's solicitor.

You may be charged extra for services or communications such as emails and telephone calls, so, before you choose one, ask several solicitors for written quotes and details about their professional fees and any other additional costs.

Use the questions below from ccpc.ie to help you compare what each solicitor can offer:

- How much do you charge for a standard conveyancing?
- What does the fee include and not include?
- Do you have a fixed fee quotation or an estimate?
- Will there be any extra fees for administration costs,

such as postage?

- Could the fee change and if so, why?
- Do you have a no-sale, no-fee policy in place?
- Will you let me know in advance if something will cost extra?
- What is the maximum I can expect to pay?
- What parts of the process will you look after?
- How long should the process take?
- How will you update me and how often?
- What do I need to do before the closing date?
- Are you a member of the Incorporated Law Society of Ireland?

> 🏠 **Good news story**
>
> Split up from my fiancé in my early thirties, thought I knew which direction my life was going. Started saving for my own house and a roof over my head. Work as a nurse and worked almost every day over Covid to save for my own place. Honestly, got very disheartened by the increasing property prices and never thought I'd get a house, let alone a house in

Dublin. But during the summer, went sale agreed on my own house in Dublin and moved in in September. So happy and loving my freedom! It's so hard but can be done.

Aoife, Dublin

ACTION STEPS

- Seek out recommendations for a solicitor from trusted sources.
- Contact at least three different solicitors with the questions provided above.

6
MORTGAGE PROTECTION AND LIFE INSURANCE

- Mortgage protection is required when buying a home in Ireland and pays off the mortgage balance if the borrower dies during the term.

- It is important to arrange mortgage protection early, as it can sometimes take longer to obtain than the mortgage itself. Payments and start date can be deferred until the mortgage is drawn down.

- Third-party options may offer better rates and value than those offered by the lender or mortgage broker.

- Mortgage protection is mandatory, covers the bank's interest, and has decreasing coverage over time. Life insurance is not mandatory, goes to the borrower's family, and has fixed coverage.

MORTGAGE protection is legally required now when buying a home: you cannot draw down your mortgage until you have mortgage protection in place. This is why I believe it is important to get this organised early in your home-buying journey. You can arrange the policy in advance and postpone the starting date until you draw down your mortgage.

I recently heard an awful story from one of my followers on Instagram who, after three years of trying, finally agreed a sale price on their home. Everything was going well until they tried to get the legally required mortgage protection only to be told they could not be covered because they had recovered from cancer two years previously. So, this person was being punished for having beaten cancer ... how horrible is that? I have heard similar horror stories from people with diabetes, cystic fibrosis, obesity and many other underlying health conditions. It's really tough hearing these stories. Things are already difficult enough for people to actually find a home to buy, to then be let down over something that is outside of their control. My advice, regardless of your previous or current medical history, is to talk to an insurance broker early on and see what your options are. Be open and honest about your health history and work with them to try and get the best cover needed.

LIFE INSURANCE VERSUS MORTGAGE PROTECTION

Life insurance

- Life insurance is a tax-free lump sum paid out to your family if you die during the term of the mortgage.
- The amount of cover is fixed.
- Life insurance costs more than mortgage protection.
- Life insurance is not mandatory.

Mortgage protection

- Mortgage protection is a tax-free cash sum that's paid out to the bank if you die, to clear off your mortgage.
- The amount of cover reduces over time.
- Mortgage protection costs less than life insurance.
- Mortgage protection is mandatory.
- The huge difference here is that life insurance goes to your partner or family, whereas mortgage protection covers your bank's back and it's unavoidable if you're buying a home in Ireland.

WHAT IS MORTGAGE PROTECTION?

Mortgage protection insurance is a type of life insurance

that you must buy when you are getting a mortgage in Ireland. If you or your partner dies during the term (years) of the mortgage, the mortgage protection policy pays off the outstanding balance on your mortgage.

At what stage do you need mortgage protection?

Sometimes, getting mortgage protection insurance may prove difficult, so apply for it as soon as possible because it can take more time than the mortgage approval itself, thereby delaying the whole process. You can get your policy set up and defer the payments and start date until you draw down your mortgage.

⊶ Top tip number 1 for mortgage protection

You do not have to take your lender or mortgage broker's policy. They will likely push you to take their policy, and say that it is far more complicated to organise your own, but they're lying. It's not more complicated and you will likely save a fortune by using a third party's service like Beat The Bank online. Disclaimer alert: I am a brand ambassador for this company but only because I believe it provides great rates and options.

🏠 **Good news story**

We were living overseas during Covid. We had been searching for a home to buy for years at home, but we often got overbid.

Then we saw a home that we liked had come back on the market. I called the agent. The agent was a family-run business who said they had a strict viewing policy and that we would have to view the house. Unfortunately, due to Covid, we were stuck in Qatar.

He said, 'I will find you another place.'

I said, 'But we like this one.'

I asked if I could have my mother come and view for me. No.

He asked me to email him and he would get back to me, so I did. I explained my situation and that I am actually from the area, who I know in the area and who I used to work for. It turned out that he went to school with a former employer and with that we were allowed to have my mother view the home for

---

us while we viewed it remotely from Doha.

We loved the house and put in an offer. After a few days of bidding the seller accepted our offer. We were beyond happy, dying to see the place – the wife had to ground me cos I got so excited that I began buying furniture online.

We managed to buy our furniture in advance remotely with the help of my mother and sisters. They were measuring and marking the floors so we could see what space we had for everything. My mother was the one who went to the furniture shop to test the sofa for us and since there was a lead time, we managed to order in advance for our return to Dublin that summer. We were delighted with our blind purchase. Our first family home.

Keith, Dublin

⚸ Top tips

- As stated above, you do not have to buy mortgage protection from the bank (no matter what the bank says). Always shop around and buy the policy that offers the best value and service.

- Buying from an insurance broker will not slow down your mortgage application (no matter what the bank says). In fact, brokers are generally quicker than banks.

- If you add serious illness cover to your mortgage protection policy, the bank, not you, will get any pay out. (This is important to know, and the bank may not tell you.) This means that your mortgage gets paid off, as it is your bank that technically owns the policy.

- Dual life cover is better than joint life cover (and they are similarly priced). Avoid joint life cover. Dual life cover is not usually available through the banks. What's the difference? Dual life can potentially have two pay outs, joint life only has one potential pay out. For example, on a €300,000 mortgage, a dual life plan has a potential pay out of €600,000, while a joint life plan has a maximum pay out of €300,000.

- If there are two people on the mortgage, you both need mortgage protection for the full value of the mortgage (not 50 per cent each).

- If you are buying as a couple but aren't married,

you should consider two single life policies to minimise potential inheritance tax liabilities.

• Your premium is fixed for the life of the policy.

• You do not need life insurance to draw-down your mortgage, no matter what your bank tells you. All you need is basic mortgage protection. This is important to know.

• You only need to insure the mortgage amount, not the purchase price of the property.

• You don't need to insure the interest payable on the mortgage, just the principal amount you are borrowing. For example, if you borrow €300,000, you only insure €300,000, not the final amount paid at the end of your mortgage term.

• If you have a health issue, speak to an insurance broker before you apply. If your bank declines you, it will be harder for you to get cover elsewhere.

• If you use e-cigarettes, the bank will charge you the same rate as a cigarette smoker (twice the price of a non-smoker). Brokers usually have access to preferential rates for vapers.

- Try to get a 'conversion' option with your policy. This means you will be able to extend your cover at any time without having to do a medical or provide more medical history. Without a 'conversion', if you have health issues in the future, those issues may prevent you from getting affordable cover when you're older.

- Finally, you cannot get exclusions on a mortgage protection policy. The insurer will either cover you for death for any reason, or will not cover you at all.

What if I cannot get mortgage protection cover?

It is still possible to get a mortgage without mortgage protection. In some circumstances, you can get a waiver, for example if you are aged over 50 or if you are buying an investment property. You might be able to get a waiver if you can prove that you're 'uninsurable'.

A refusal from three different insurers will usually be enough to prove that you cannot obtain insurance. Unfortunately, some lenders will still reject your application, but it is worth a try and it's a good idea to have a discussion with your mortgage broker or mortgage advisor on whether a lender will give you a waiver or not. Please note: If you die without a mortgage protection insurance policy in place, the responsibility for paying off the mortgage will fall to your beneficiaries, if you have any. If the mortgage is not paid off, your beneficiaries may have to sell the property in order to pay off the debt.

Policy assignment

When you do purchase mortgage protection insurance, it is important to know that the policy will be assigned to your bank or lender. This is called a 'deed of assignment'. In other words, the bank or lender then own the insurance policy, not you, as they are the ones who will be paid in the event of a death.

Once your policy has been finalised, your insurer will send what's called a 'confirmation of assignment' letter to your bank. This is one of the steps needed to draw down your mortgage and finally be able to move into your new home.

Do I need to have a medical examination?

Usually not. But like most things, it depends, and in this case, it depends on your general level of health. As mentioned previously, there may be issues if you have a history of illness. Sometimes, the insurance company will send a medical questionnaire to your doctor.

Your life insurance company may also have a medical questionnaire sent to your doctor for him or her to complete.

Mortgage protection can be confusing, and I am not a qualified advisor so I would highly recommend talking to a dedicated insurance broker to find the cover that best suits you. You just need to know that basic mortgage protection is all that is legally required to draw down your mortgage. You do not have to have life insurance but lenders are legally required to ensure that you have a mortgage protection policy in place so that the bank is repaid in the event of your death. Grim, I know.

ACTION STEPS

- Make sure to apply for mortgage protection early in your home-buying journey.
- Compare policies from your bank with what an insurance broker has to offer.
- See if dual life suits your situation best.
- Get a 'conversion' option with your policy.

CURRENT GOVERNMENT SCHEMES

7

- Help to Buy Scheme
- First Home Scheme
- Living City Initiative
- Croí Cónaithe
- Local Authority Home Loan

THE government has a number of schemes that have been implemented to make buying a home more affordable for you. I am sceptical of schemes like 'Help to Buy' and the new 'First Home Scheme' as these, in my opinion, are demand-side schemes (these schemes increase demand on housing by increasing buyers' potential to spend, i.e. helping with the deposit or giving grants) and not only do nothing to increase supply but also serve to prop up already record-high house prices. Demand-side housing schemes like these do not address the issue of limited housing supply and therefore may not greatly benefit homebuyers because they do not increase the number of homes available for purchase. However, these schemes are in place and if they can help you then you may as well make use of them. Do keep in mind that the government regularly makes changes to these so I would advise you check out revenue.ie for up-to-date information.

HTB: HELP TO BUY SCHEME

This scheme allows you to claim up to €30,000 off the price of a new home and has certain conditions attached. It is only available to first-time buyers, is only available on new-build or self-build homes and you must live in the home for five years after purchasing. The HTB scheme was introduced to help people get a deposit for their home. It is not available on existing homes already built. HTB is a tax refund scheme based on any income tax that you have paid over the previous four years. So, if you haven't been working or paying tax for the full four years, you will not be able to avail of the full €30,000. Here are the details for availing of HTB at the time of writing, which is subject to change.

- You must be a first-time buyer.

- You must be buying or building a brand-new home.

- You must be taking out a mortgage for a minimum of 70 per cent of the value of the property.

- The property must not be worth more than €500,000.

- You may qualify for either of the following: 10 per cent of the purchase or build price, or €30,000, whichever is lower.

- You must apply online through myAccount on revenue.ie and your tax affairs must be up to date.

How will the refund be paid?

The refund gets paid to the developer or contractor and they must be registered with the scheme. If you are doing a self-build, the refund will be paid to a bank account you hold with your loan provider.

How do you apply for HTB?

It is all done through revenue.ie so you must have an account set up. If you are self-employed or self-assessed you must have a tax clearance certificate, among other things.

The following is taken directly from the revenue.ie website.

There are three stages to the online process:

- Application stage
- Claim stage
- Verification stage

Application stage

Before starting your application, please ensure you are tax compliant. You can apply as an individual or as part of a group.

Use myAccount or Revenue Online Service (ROS) to apply. Complete the declaration and select the years you wish to use for a refund. If you are tax compliant, your application will be approved, and you will be given:

- An application number
- A summary of the maximum amount you can claim
- An access code (sent through MyEnquiries)

Keep a safe note of these numbers, you may need to provide them to your lender, contractor or solicitor at the verification stage.

Note: Even if your application is approved, all conditions of the Help to Buy (HTB) scheme must be satisfied for the claim to be approved. A valid claim must be submitted before the application expires, otherwise your application will have to be resubmitted. Applications made between:

- 1 January and 30 September automatically expire on 31 December of the same year
- 1 October and 31 December automatically expire on 31 March of the following year

Lenders and contractors can use Revenue's mortgage query tool to check your potential maximum HTB refund.

Claim stage

You can make your claim using ROS or myAccount once your application is approved, and all other conditions are satisfied.

Step 1: Upload evidence of your mortgage and, if you are:

- Purchasing a new property, upload a copy of the contract, signed and dated by the vendor and all purchasers

- Self-building, upload proof of the draw down of the first part of the mortgage and a copy of the valuation report from your lender.

Step 2: You need to confirm details about the:

- Property: purchase value (if you are purchasing a property) or approved valuation (if you are self-building)
- Date of completion
- Mortgage
- Amount of deposit already paid
- If you are applying with other people, you will also need to confirm the portion of the refund due to each person
- If you are self-building, you will need to provide the BIC and IBAN of the relevant bank account held with your mortgage provider.

Once you have submitted your claim, you will be provided with a claim number. If you enter incorrect information during your application or claim, you must cancel it. You can then submit a new application or claim before continuing to the next stage.

Verification stage

Before you receive any refund, the information you have provided will need to be verified by your:

- Qualifying contractor, if you are purchasing a property
- Solicitor, if you are self-building

When you have submitted your claim, advise your eligible verifier and provide them with your:

- Claim number (issued after the claim stage) and access code (issued when your application was approved)

The refund that you receive is limited to 10 per cent of the purchase value or approved valuation. This may mean that it is different to the maximum relief amount advised at the application stage.

Can Revenue claw back a refund?

Revenue can claw back refunds if you:

- Were not entitled to the refund
- Do not live in the property for a minimum of five years
- Did not finish the process to purchase the property

- Did not finish building the property.

Revenue can claw back refunds from the contractor if:

- The property is not purchased by you within two years from when the refund was made to the contractor
- Revenue has reasonable grounds to believe that the property will not be purchased by you within that two-year period.

There is some flexibility around the two-year period. This can apply if Revenue is satisfied that the property is either:

- Almost complete at the end of the two years
- Likely to be completed within a reasonable time period

Once the property is completed and purchased by you, you are solely responsible for meeting the conditions for the Help to Buy refund. The developer is no longer responsible after this point.

FHS: FIRST HOME SCHEME (SHARED EQUITY)

This scheme again only applies to new-build homes and

essentially means the government will give you money on top of the amount you have mortgage approval for, to make up the difference to buy your home. This means the government will own a certain percentage of your home. It can also be used in combination with the Help to Buy scheme. Instead of the value of this scheme being a rigid amount, it is linked as a percentage of the value of the home as house prices can go up and down.

For example, let's say there's a new-build house for sale in Dublin for €450,000.

- Joint application from a first-time buyer couple with a combined income of: €87,500
- Maximum amount they can borrow: €350,000
- Deposit saved: €15,000
- Help To Buy: €30,000
- Shortfall that could be met using FHS: €55,000 (which is 12.2 per cent).

So, in this example the government could give the couple €55,000 so they can buy the new-build home. This 'loan' is interest-free for the first five years and after that the interest rates start to go up. The couple can then choose to buy out the government's equity stake or not. It is worth remembering that the government has a 12.2 per cent stake in the home, rather than €55,000, as the value of the home may increase or decrease.

The below is taken directly from the government's own website, firsthomescheme.ie.

Eligibility

To be eligible for the scheme you must:

- Be over 18 years of age
- Be a first-time buyer or other eligible homebuyer
- Have a mortgage approval with a participating lender*
- Borrow the maximum amount available to you from one of the participating lenders (up to four times your income)
- Not be availing of a macro prudential exception (MPE) with a participating lender; that is, you cannot already be in receipt of any sort of exemption
- Have a minimum deposit of 10 per cent of the property purchase price, including any contribution from HTB.

To be eligible for the scheme the property you are purchasing must:

- Be a newly built house or apartment in a private development in the Republic of Ireland
- Be bought as your principal private residence
- Be within the local authority property price ceiling for the property type (house or apartment)
- Not be a self-build (although there is talk of this condition being removed).

To see if you could qualify for FHS support, you can use the eligibility calculator on firsthomescheme.ie.

*A participating lender is an authorised mortgage lender that invests in the First Home Scheme and becomes a shareholder in the properties it helps to fund. In order to be eligible for the FHS, you must take out a mortgage with a participating lender. At the time of writing, the participating lenders are:

- Allied Irish Banks plc (including AIB, Haven Mortgages, and EBS)
- Bank of Ireland Group plc • Permanent TSB plc.

How much funding can the FHS provide?

The FHS can fund up to 30 per cent of the market value of your new property.

This amount is reduced to 20 per cent if you are availing of the Help to Buy scheme (HTB). Further details of HTB can be found on Revenue's website (www.revenue.ie), and examples, including the HTB, can be found in the Homebuyer's Guide on the Guides/Resources page on firsthomescheme.ie.

The minimum equity share is 2.5 per cent of the property purchase price, or €10,000, whichever is higher.

Do I need to pay the equity facility back?

The FHS is not a loan and doesn't need to be paid back, except in the following circumstances known as mandatory redemption events.

- The property is sold
- The property is no longer your principal private residence
- You move or switch your mortgage to a non-participating lender

- If you die (or, in the case of joint applications, the last applicant dies).

However, you can choose to redeem part or all of the equity facility whenever you like.

What about fees and charges?

Service charges will be applied to your account from the start of year six, as payment to the FHS for services related to the provision, maintenance and servicing of the equity facility.

Service charges are fixed for the life of the equity and are calculated at the following rates per annum:

Years	Service Charge Rate
0–5	0%
6–15	1.75%
16–29	2.15%

Property prices can go up and down. As the equity is linked to the value of your home, any change in property prices will affect any partial or final redemption amounts. If property prices increase or decrease over time, the percentage equity you have to redeem will remain the same but the euro amount will increase or decrease.

See an example in the case of a price increase below.

- Customer purchases a property for €250,000, availing of €25,000 from the First Home Scheme (FHS) which means the FHS has a 10 per cent FHS equity share in the home. At a point in the future, the customer decides to buy out the FHS equity share. The home is now valued at €350,000. As the FHS equity share is unchanged at 10 per cent, the customer will now need €35,000 plus any accrued service charges payable, to redeem the FHS equity share in the home.

Price caps

There are different price caps depending on where the home is located and what type of home it is. See the tables below.

Local Authority Area	Price Limits
Cork City, Dublin City, Dún Laoghaire-Rathdown, Fingal, South Dublin	€475,000 for houses and €500,000 for apartments
Galway City	€425,000 for houses and €450,000 for apartments

Limerick City and County	€375,000 for houses and €450,000 for apartments
Waterford City and County	€350,000 for houses and €450,000 for apartments
Co Wicklow	€475,000 for all properties
Co Cork, Co Kildare	€425,000 for all properties
Co Galway, Co Kilkenny, Co Louth, Co Meath, Co Westmeath	€375,000 for all properties
Co Laois	€350,000 for all properties
Co Carlow, Co Cavan, Co Clare, Co Donegal, Co Kerry, Co Leitrim, Co Longford, Co Mayo, Co Monaghan, Co Offaly, Co Roscommon, Co Sligo, Co Tipperary, Co Wexford	€325,000 for all properties

Duplexes are classed as houses so fall within the 'house price ceiling'

🏠 Good news story

First-time buyers, after years of grafting and saving, including a year of living in a parents' shed (which then turned out to be nearly four years, thanks Covid) my other half was put on the wage subsidy scheme (WSS). Hurrah for the hospitality sector! We were told by banks that while on this, we would not be entertained for a mortgage.

Thanks to CHP and your followers' comments we found a few providers that would overlook the WSS. Back on track.

Eventually, we were finalising our approval process,

all going smoothly with a number of house viewings under our belt, but house prices were rocketing, especially in Dublin where we are both from and wanted to buy.

Approval in hand, the excitement of house hunting helping us forget about the disaster that was Covid and then ... more surprising news added to this house buying adventure: a little baby boy was due to arrive in a short few months.

This left us with very little time to find a house, bid on it, get solicitors and documentation finalised before we would have to tell the mortgage provider that we would have another human under our potential new roof, and possibly starting our approval process all over again!

Our search area now sprawled over counties. A lovely three-bed, semi-detached in Naas caught our eye. The two of us plus bump were the first viewers, loved the house and the area and stuck a cheeky, lowball offer in. To our surprise, the estate agent said if we met in the middle between our offer and asking, they would accept. Below asking price too.

They loved the fact that we were a young family

looking to settle into our first home, which we reiterated a number of times as per CHP tips to promote families and demote investors.

After some long months of solicitor back and forth, some outdated planning permission slowing things down and causing minor panic with new mammy now without wage slips to show the mortgage provider, we are now happily settled in after gutting the house and making it our own. Baby and all.

Thanks CHP and followers for the advice, and more importantly the reassurance that we weren't alone in the barrage of hurdles and hardships along the way.

Paul, Kildare

There are a number of scenarios that could potentially play out with the FHS. Property values could decrease or increase, or you could buy a portion of the equity back. I would recommend you go through the resources on the First Homes Scheme website rigorously to assess whether this scheme is worthwhile for you or not.

LAHL: LOCAL AUTHORITY HOME LOAN

The Local Authority Home Loan (LAHL) is a government-backed mortgage for first-time buyers or other eligible applicants* through local authorities. You can use this mortgage to buy a new or existing home and for self-builds. It also includes the purchase of homes through state schemes such as the Tenant Purchase Scheme and Affordable Housing Schemes, with the exception of the First Home Scheme.

*The 'Fresh Start Principle' affords people who are divorced or separated and have no interest in the previous family home, or who have undergone personal insolvency or bankruptcy arrangement or proceedings or other legal process, eligibility to apply.

To qualify for this, you need to have been refused a mortgage from two lenders. You can use the LAHL to borrow up to 90 per cent of the value of the home. The loan works like any other mortgage loan and you pay it via a monthly direct debit. There are some maximum values:

- €320,000 in the counties of Cork, Dublin, Galway, Kildare, Louth, Meath and Wicklow

- €250,000 in the rest of the country

The following is taken from the LAHL website. To be eligible for a LAHL, you must:

- Be a first-time buyer with the exception of applicants qualifying under the Fresh Start Principle and those who have inherited residential property
- Be aged between 18 and 70 years
- Be in continuous employment for a minimum of two years, as the primary earner, or be in continuous employment for a minimum of one year, as a secondary earner
- As a single applicant have an annual gross income of not more than €65,000 in counties Cork, Dublin, Galway, Kildare, Louth, Meath and Wicklow and be earning under €50,000 (gross) in all other counties
- As joint applicants have an annual gross income of not more than €75,000 in all counties
- Submit certified accounts for two years if self-employed
- Provide proof of insufficient mortgage offers of finance from two regulated financial providers

- Not be a current or previous owner of residential property in or outside the Republic of Ireland, unless you are a 'Fresh Start' applicant
- Declare that you are a first-time buyer. You must authorise the local authority to conduct such checks as are necessary to confirm this, such as carrying out a local property tax check.
- Occupy the property as your normal place of residence
- Purchase or self-build a property situated in the Republic of Ireland
- Purchase or self-build a property which does not exceed the maximum market value applicable for the county in which it is located
- Consent to a central credit register check
- Currently have a legal right to reside and work in the state and be able to demonstrate that you are habitually resident in Ireland.

Eligibility is subject to submission of a complete Local Authority Home Loan application form and confirmation by your local authority.

Interest rates

A Local Authority Home Loan offers two fixed interest rate products:

- 3.35 per cent fixed for up to 25 years (APR 3.4 per cent)*

- 3.45 per cent fixed for up to 30 years (APR 3.51 per cent)*

*Rates are subject to change. Mortgage rates are set on the date of drawdown of your loan.

All rates are exclusive of mortgage protection insurance (MPI) which is a requirement of borrowing. Eligible borrowers are required to partake in the local authority collective MPI scheme. MPI is payable monthly, in addition to loan repayments.

I have received many messages from followers about this. Apparently the MPI scheme that you must use when getting a LAHL is extremely expensive in comparison to other providers. One person told me their MPI is €150 per month, while my mortgage protection is only €25 per month. When you add that €125 difference up over the term of the mortgage, it equates to €45,000.

There are pros and cons with the LAHL. One of the main benefits of the LAHL is the low interest rates with long fixed-term rates. This means you know exactly what your monthly repayments will be for the entire period and you can budget accordingly. With the current market and interest rates going up, the LAHL rates appear to be very good. However, if you ever want to switch to another mortgage provider, you may be liable for a breakage fee. You also cannot overpay your mortgage, i.e. pay it off sooner than the term of the loan, without paying a fee for doing so.

One of the biggest issues is the mortgage protection insurance (MPI) scheme, and this is not something you can change. I believe it is around 0.55 per cent of the loan. Here is an example.

- Loan amount: €200,000
- 0.55 per cent = €1,100 per year

In this case, the monthly MPI payment would be €91.66 which is a lot in comparison to other providers. So, you need to do the sums to work out if the lower interest rates over the 25 or 30 years is worth it while considering how much you will be paying monthly for mortgage protection.

🏠 Good news story

We probably didn't have the hardest or longest journey but it sure wasn't easy either. We couldn't get enough money from the banks due to our salaries so we went down the Local Authority Home Loan scheme, a process which is nearly as slow and painful as house hunting itself. Like everyone, we were outbid again and again. Then we found our perfect home in Rush for €342,000, we were elated. That was until we were told by the county council that we couldn't spend a penny over €320,000 and had to let the house go. Fast forward three weeks later and we find another house in Rush that we like, only to end up in a bidding war with an investor. Thankfully, they weren't willing to pay more than us. We moved in two weeks ago and directly across the road is the perfect home we missed out on. You couldn't make it up! We're more than happy with what we have though. Had we not secured this place, I think we would have been priced out of Dublin. Truthfully, it really was now or never for us. Your page kept me sane and made me believe that we could get a house in a time when it was impossible to believe. Thanks Ciarán, you really are one of the good ones!

Jen, Dublin

OTHER SCHEMES AROUND PROPERTY

If, like me, you are likely priced out of new-builds and might be looking to take on a 'fixer-upper' home, the government does have some good schemes that can help with renovation costs. It is important to keep in mind that at the time of writing, material and building costs are at record highs. This is down to a combination of rising inflation and a lack of available labour. There is still some value to be found in a 'fixer-upper' though, especially if you're willing to take on some of the work yourself or have good connections with people in trades like carpentry, electrics and plumbing. I won't go into huge detail on these schemes as they are more applicable after buying a home but there is a lot of information available on them over on revenue.ie.

Living City Initiative (LCI)

The Living City Initiative (LCI) is a scheme to help claw back some of the costs of renovating an old house by giving tax returns. You can claim 10 per cent of the cost as a deduction from your total income each year for ten years. There is a minimum of €5,000 and no upper limit for the amount you spend. In order to qualify, your property needs to be within very specific 'special regeneration areas' and have been built before 1915.

There are three types of relief available under the LCI.

- Owner-occupier residential relief
- Rented residential (landlord) relief
- Commercial relief

LCI is only available within certain areas of the following cities:

- Dublin
- Limerick
- Cork
- Galway
- Waterford
- Kilkenny

There is help available with this, and good advice. If you decide to go down this route, a multi-disciplinary, free advisory team from planning, architects, fire prevention, building control, conservation, valuers and other relevant departments is available to meet with you and run through any queries or questions you have in relation to the planning process, compliance with regulations or fire safety requirements. There is no charge for this service.

Croí Cónaithe

Under this scheme, you may be able to claim a grant of up to €50,000 to help with renovation costs of a vacant or derelict property. The home must be used as your primary residence, which I think is great as it means it is aimed at owner-occupiers rather than investors. The Croí Cónaithe scheme is not limited to residential property, and can be used to convert what was previously a commercial property into a primary residence, for example buying an old pub and turning it into a home.

To qualify for a €30,000 grant, the property must have been vacant for two years or more and have been built before 1997. If the works are set to cost more than €30,000, there is an additional €20,000 grant available but you will have to prove that the property is not just vacant, but also derelict. The definition of derelict can be something of a grey area but Revenue say it must be 'structurally unsound and dangerous'. This can be confirmed by an engineer in a report. You will have to prove the property was vacant for at least two years by using utility bills or some other method approved by the local authority.

This is a relatively new scheme and the details are still being worked out. At the moment, it is only available for towns with a population of 400 or more people and the property must have walkable access to a town or village via a pathway but I imagine these limitations will soon be removed and it will be open to any home. One of the good things about this scheme is that it is available to all buyers, not just FTBs. As it is a new scheme, I have not yet received any stories from people who have been able to avail of it, but hopefully it can help you if this is the type of home you are interested in. Personally, I have always wanted to own an old pub in the countryside!

CONCLUSION

That is all the government schemes available at present, but more could be announced any time. You will notice that a lot of the above schemes only apply to new-builds. It could be argued that the schemes are there to help private developers and continue to prop up already extremely high house prices. I have been critical of the HTB scheme over the years as it has been shown to increase new-build house prices and is poorly targeted: most people that used it had already saved a deposit. The same criticisms have been shared by the Economic and Social Research Institute (ESRI) about the FHS and a similar scheme in the UK was heavily criticised by housing and economic experts. However, these are broader, macroeconomic issues and beyond the scope of this book.

The fact is these schemes are here and they are available and if they can help you buy your home, then you may as well make use of them.

ACTION STEPS

- Research each scheme in detail and decide if any of them are suitable for you.
- Check for the most up-to-date information on revenue.ie and citizensinformation.ie as the details for each scheme change regularly.

HOW TO RESEARCH A HOME

- RESEARCHING homes online can save time and hassle by allowing you to identify potential deal-breakers before committing to viewings.

- Google Maps is a useful tool for finding out about public transport, commuting times, and neighbourhood features such as the size of gardens and presence of extensions.

- The Irish Property Price Register (PPR) is a useful resource for finding out how much a home has previously sold for, but does not provide detailed information about the home.

- SpeakingSame and Daft.ie can provide additional information about a home, including old photos and details about the size and number of bedrooms.

- It is also helpful to research the local schools, public transport, and local amenities in the area.

🏠 Good news story

We drove around a lot during lockdown when we were allowed to and found old houses that were in liveable condition. We put flyers through the doors saying we were starting off on the property ladder, we had seven children and had a lot to contribute to the area. We told our story of our family and all we wanted was a home of our own.

We had three calls inside the first week. We went to see one house and within seconds the owners fell in love with us and our family. We loved the area, our children would keep a second teacher in the school of 15 children, the GAA team were getting extra kids. We agreed on our price. A week later with zero money handed over, the seller gave us the keys of the house and told us start decorating and move in when we wanted.

We moved in one week later. It took one week to modernise the house, we drew down our mortgage, two solicitors worked away in the background with zero stress or hassle and a few weeks later we officially were homeowners. The seller gave my husband full-time work in his construction company when he saw how much improvements we made in one week. And to top it all off, when we were saying to him we were saving for new windows and doors, he handed us €5,000 and told us he was never as glad to have a family in it, that we're going to add to the community and keep a school open, and love the house as much as he did.

It's not modern or super fancy but it is our own and our mortgage is €387 a month. Our children help him farm his land at the weekends – his farmyard is right across from our house so we see him regularly. He took a chance on us and we took a chance on him and it worked out wonderfully for us. We got our house for an amazing price from a man who just wanted to see life in the rural area again, and with seven children we brought plenty of life to the area.

Catherine, Sligo

One of the many benefits of the internet is that you have access to free websites that can help you research pretty much anything, and researching your home is no different. In this chapter I will run through the process that I used to research houses in-depth to figure out if they were the right home for us. You might have certain 'must-haves' in your home-hunting criteria, for example you may want to be able to extend your home down the line. This can all be figured out from the comfort of your couch, and it won't cost you a cent.

The benefit of this research is that it can save you the hassle of taking time off work to go to viewings only to be let down by a deal-breaker like the garden being too small or having no amenities within walking distance. It can also stop you getting your hopes up when you think you've found the perfect home only to realise it's not suitable for your needs because there are no schools in the area or the public transport is rubbish. The following can be done in any order, and should only take 30 minutes to figure out everything you need to know.

PROPERTY TAX

Google 'Revenue calculate your local property tax' and click on the first result that comes up. This brings you to the search box on revenue.ie where you simply put in the details of the home you're looking at and it will tell you how much the property tax is on that home. Property taxes in Ireland are cheap in comparison to other countries, so it shouldn't end up being a deal-breaker but it is good to know how much you'll need to pay each year.

GOOGLE MAPS

Bit of an obvious one here but Google Maps is an amazing resource for a huge amount of information. Not just for figuring out public transport, but also, for example, to see if other people nearby have added two-storey extensions to their house. This shows a precedent for such an extension and means you are likely to get approval if you wanted one in the future. Here are some of my favourite features of Google Maps.

⌐ Google Maps top tips

- Figuring out your commute to and from work. You can change the settings in the directions so that you can set the 'departure' time or the 'arrive by' time, which is really handy for figuring out how long a journey will take during rush-hour traffic.

- Public transport. You could put in your most frequent or favourite destinations (pub, restaurant, gym, etc) and click on the public transport tab and it will show you which services are nearby (buses, trains, Luas) and even when they are due. One great feature tells you how busy buses are: if there are seats or if there is just space for standing. It is also good for estimating how long a walk or cycle would be, although I find the estimations are generally longer than they actually take.

- Satellite view. Change the settings to see the landscape around the home. This is helpful to see the size of gardens and if other houses have driveways or extensions. You can also use this to check the orientation of the house and where the sun will rise and set. Will the garden get sun? Use suncalc.org and put in the address, this will tell you exactly when and where the sun will hit. Super handy tool!

- Street view. Highly recommend you use this and go for a virtual walk around the place. Street view is updated regularly and can give you an insight into what is happening around the area. Also, if you search on desktop, you can flick through the history of street view which gives you a good timeline of changes in the place. When I search my own house I can see as far back as 2009, but this may vary depending on where in the country the home is and how often the Google Maps car has visited.

Property Price Register (PPR) propertypriceregister.ie

This will be one of your most used websites when home-hunting. I always recommend people search the PPR to see what the home has sold for previously (if available). The register goes back as far as 2010. If the property is a new-build, the price shown will be exclusive of VAT at 13.5 per cent which is worth remembering. The only downside to the PPR is that it doesn't give you much information in terms of the details of the home, floor space, the number of bedrooms and so on, but there may be ways to get around this.

SPEAKINGSAME (IR.SPEAKINGSAME.COM)

Occasionally, you can search a property's address on SpeakingSame and it will bring up old photos or other details. This sort of information is not always available, but with some navigating you can often find useful information such as old photos from earlier sales of the same home. Then, you can compare these to the most recent photos and see if any work has been done to the home.

ARCHIVE.ORG

This is a handy one for old websites. If you have managed to find an old URL (say, from an email alert) and the website is now dead, you can put it into archive.org and it will show you that website. You may also get lucky and turn up a cached page on a Google search.

MYPLAN.IE

This is a fantastic website that can give you a huge amount of information on everything from planning permissions to future developments in the area. Always a good one to check to see what kind of large-scale construction might be going on around the home: you might not want to live next to a construction site for five years. You can also see what planning permissions have been granted or rejected in neighbouring homes. You can even see architect drawings and all other documents relating to a planning permission application. MyPlan.ie is colour coded to make things easier to navigate. It is very useful if you're looking at a home that you hope to extend in the future: by checking other people's planning permissions in the area, not only can you get an idea if your planning application will be approved, but you can also get inspiration from other people's applications and drawings.

LANDDIRECT.IE

This one is similar enough to myplan.ie but you can use landdirect.ie to check if the home is leasehold or freehold.

To access the database, click on 'proceed as guest' and enter the property's address. This website works best on desktop. You can also check who owns a property via the land registry. It costs €5 to do a search and it provides you with the name of the person who currently owns the home. So, let's say there is a derelict property you are interested in and would like to buy directly from the owner. Input all relevant information into the land registry directory and pay €5 for the details you need. I've heard from a number of people who have had good success with this method.

FLOODINFO.IE

Unfortunately, with the climate crisis, I think this website is going to get more and more use over the next few years. Here, you can check the flooding history of the area the home is in and what the future risks of flooding are. This is important because being in a floodzone can make insuring your home almost impossible. And if the property is in an area prone to flooding, your lender may not let you buy the home as you will probably not be able to insure it. There are ways to overcome this but it's best to talk to your solicitor, lender or insurance broker for better advice.

SEAI.IE

The Sustainable Energy Authority of Ireland's website was great for information on the running costs of a home and potential renovation costs. It was a huge help to us when we retrofitted our house and it contains a vast amount of information. You can investigate any grants available and the average running costs of a home depending on its BER rating. If you have the BER certificate number of a house for sale, you can access the full report via the search function on the SEAI website. Go to 'find an existing BER' and enter the number there. The advisory report will show the home's performance as well as an accurate floor area. If the home you're looking at has a very poor BER rating, you know it is going to cost a lot of money to run each month. Especially now as energy prices are on the rise.

The SEAI website has a full list of grants available. There are different grants available depending on whether you want to use individual grants or go down the 'one stop shop' route. For example, if you live in a semi-detached or end-of-terrace house, you can get a grant of €1,300 towards insulating your attic. A huge amount of heat is lost through the attic, so insulating it is relatively cheap and will make a big difference to the heat retention of your home.

RIAI.IE

This website will give you a decent guide as to how much construction and renovation costs will be on a given home. The prices in the brochure 'Working with an Architect' are from 2019 so a little dated as of writing, but they can give a good guide as to how much the home you're looking at may cost to renovate or extend. This is always a difficult one to price as it will depend on the level of skill you have yourself and how much work you're willing to do. There are lots of other useful guides on the site and again, it is all free.

COMPARISON WEBSITES

Websites like bonkers.ie and switcher.ie are brilliant for inputting a property's address and comparing what suppliers are available for broadband and TV, as well as the speeds available at the address.

MOBILE PHONE COVERAGE

Head to comreg.ie/tools-resources and you will find the coverage map to see what the signal will be like on each network at the home's address. You can also use this to compare phone, broadband and TV prices. The coverage map is really important because it is incredibly irritating not having good phone signal when you're at home.

RADON

According to the Environmental Protection Agency (EPA), 'Radon is a radioactive gas that causes lung cancer. It is formed in the ground by the radioactive decay of uranium which is present in all rocks and soils. You cannot see it, smell it or taste it. It can only be measured with special detectors. Radon can cause lung cancer when exposed to high levels over a long period of time. Every year in Ireland, radon causes about 350 cases of lung cancer.'

If you google 'radon map coverage' and go to the first

result you will see the Environmental Protection Agency website (I advise this approach as the radon map is difficult to find from the EPA homepage) and here you can input a property's eircode to find out its level of radon risk. It may come up with '1 in 20 homes here are at risk of high radon levels'. You can then get a test done if required. I am not an expert on radon so it's best to check with a professional.

There you have all of my best tips for when it comes to researching a home. If you're not familiar with an area, I advise you to visit it at multiple times throughout a day to get a proper feel for it. Take a walk around in the morning, afternoon and evening on both a weekday and a weekend to fully appreciate the atmosphere of the area. Buying a home is the biggest purchase of your life, take the time to do your research and to really understand if a particular home is the one for you.

🏠 **Good news story**

I moved out of Dublin to the midlands to rent initially, as it was impossible as a single buyer to purchase a house I wanted, in an area I wanted to live in, in

Dublin. The commute was under an hour, so I decided that my town was actually an ideal location for me.

Fast forward to some plumbing problems in my rental, and when the plumber called out, I mentioned I wanted to buy a house, and coincidentally, he was looking to sell his house. I went for a viewing (only my second house to view), and the house was incredible. Ticked all my boxes and boxes I didn't know I wanted ticked – actual dream home! We agreed a market price, which included white goods and some furniture to get me started.

We stayed in contact throughout the buying process, becoming daily towards closing, which meant we both knew where we were, and made the process totally stress free. As a bonus, as the house was rated BER B1, I managed to get a green fixed-rate mortgage [green mortgages are explained later] for four years at 1.9 per cent with Bank of Ireland, right before the interest rates shot up.

I'm in the house two months now, and could not be happier, especially as I got two kittens, David and

Annabelle, four days after moving in.

The advice received by Ciaran was invaluable. He set out the whole house-buying process in an uncomplicated way and made excellent recommendations to save money.

Claire, Laois

ACTION STEPS

- Bookmark the property price register on your web browser, you will use it a lot.
- Dedicate some time to research each home you're interested in using the websites listed in this chapter.
- Seek professional advice where necessary, check out home insurance costs in a flood risk area, for example.

9

HOW TO ENQUIRE ABOUT A HOME

- Research the home and area thoroughly before enquiring to an estate agent.

- Consider using a 'buyer's CV' to present yourself as the best candidate to the estate agent.

- Contact the specific agent handling the property by phone and follow up with an email.

- Negotiate with the seller or estate agent, including making a personal connection and demonstrating a willingness to move quickly.

- Use a solicitor to protect your interests and ensure a smooth transaction.

OVER the years I have become acquainted with a few estate agents (and believe it or not, they're not all bad) and they have given me so much insider's knowledge on how to go about things from a potential buyer's perspective.

Depending on how the market is at the time of reading (at the time of writing, it is still very much a seller's market but things are beginning to turn), you may need to adapt your approach on enquiring about homes for sale. If it is a seller's market, that means there's far more demand for homes than there are homes for sale. This means estate agents will be busy with far more enquiries per property. If it has become a buyer's market, you will have a little more power and choice over how to go about your enquiry. Assuming it is still a seller's market (I can't see 100,000 homes being built between the time of writing and time of reading), these are my best tips for making sure your enquiry stands out from the others.

BEFORE ENQUIRING

It's all about research. This is where you'll realise just how important the previous chapter is. Estate agents like to know that a potential buyer is well researched, informed and ready to make their lives easier. The thing estate agents fear most (other than my page) is a sale falling through. It's bad for their image, bad for business and a real waste of time for everyone. So, make sure your research is done. If you're serious about the home you're enquiring about, make sure you've followed all of the steps in the previous chapter. Know how much comparable homes in the area have sold for recently; this will give you a good idea if the home you're interested in is priced appropriately or not. Some agents use a tactic I like to call 'bidfishing', like catfishing, but with houses. This is when they purposely advertise a house for a lot less than what they know it's worth. They do this because they know that statistically, a home that has more people actively bidding on it will often go to a higher price than a home with fewer bidders. They are fishing for bidders to stimulate a frenzy, pushing the price up well above what it's actually worth. If you do your research, using the property price register, you'll be able to spot these types of potential situations.

HOW TO ENQUIRE

Call first, don't email. When the supply of homes is low, agents can be inundated with enquiries about what few homes they do have for sale. Find out which particular agent is dealing with the property and call them directly. This will mean you're more likely to get a direct response. In the phone call, you want to present yourself as an organised, informed buyer who is ready to move quickly on the home with little to no risk of the sale falling through. Let them know you've done your research. Afterwards, follow up your phone call with an email reminding them of who you are and what you spoke about on the phone.

🏘 Good news story

Two FTBs in our twenties with two kids. Followed the page for about a year and got so many mortgage and house-hunting tips. Spotted our dream bungalow on the market for about €20,000 over our budget (€325,000). Went in with a low offer of €290,000 thinking we'd be long priced out of it. The lady selling came back to us and asked if it was a family buying. When we confirmed we were she agreed to take the property off the market at €300,000! Truly a dream and we are hoping to have keys before Christmas. The best Christmas surprise for our kids who have waited so long not to have to share a bedroom!

Rebecca, Louth

YOUR BUYER'S CV

Present yourself as the best candidate to the agent. Have everything ready to go, and if the home is a fixer-upper, show you understand that there are works required and that you won't be surprised at the surveying stage. If you really love the home, tell the agent this. Agents like to know that you're serious and focused on one particular home and not looking at lots of others. Help yourself stand out from others by letting the agent know you have all of the following in place:

- Fully underwritten mortgage approval
- Proof of funds (but remember, don't show the exact amount)
- Mortgage protection cover ready to commence
- Solicitor in place
- No chain, you're not depending on selling another home to buy this one (if you're a first-time buyer or cash buyer)
- Surveyor organised and ready to go.

You could also take this chance to let the agent know

more about you and your situation. Explain why you love this home, what connection you have to the area, whether it will be a family home, if you are trying to live near your family, and so on. Some sellers may want to sell to owner-occupiers rather than an investor, so let the agent know your plans and they may mention this to the sellers.

BUILD A RAPPORT

Estate agents can have a big influence on a seller and advise them on their decision. It's not always about the highest offer. I have hundreds of examples on my page of people being successful in bidding despite not being the highest bidder simply because their sale was more likely to go through because they had everything organised and in place. If the agent knows you're organised and more likely to follow through without any hassle, then you might be chosen over someone else. And even if you're not successful with this home, there's a high chance you might have to deal with the same agent again on another home. It is always worthwhile building as good a rapport with them as you can.

ACTION STEPS

- Do your research on the home.

- Call first, then email.

- Have your buyer's CV ready.

- Build a good rapport with the agent.

10
HOW TO VIEW A HOME

- Make sure to have a journal or some way of having all your questions at hand that you want to ask at a viewing.
- Make note of the list of things to look out for, e.g. flood risk, renovations needed, etc.

THIS is when things start to get a little exciting. I am one of those nosey people who absolutely loves getting a look inside other people's homes, I think a lot of us are like that. It's why property shows are so popular. But it's also the start of this whole home-buying process starting to feel 'real'. It is exciting, but viewing homes can also become a drag, especially when you're trying to schedule viewings around a busy work schedule. A lot of agents will do viewings on a Saturday but some won't, so you'll have to figure all of that out as it comes. There's a strange feeling you get when you enter these homes, kind of like a weird nervousness mixed with excitement, which changes the more houses you view. I always felt that some were 'not right' straight away while others felt like they could be our future family home. I won't be a cliché and say you know 'the one' right away, as I don't think you do, but when we went to view the home we ended up buying (off-market, in a private sale, directly from the family) we did know right away this was the one for us. Clichés have truth to them. However, because of our research, we knew the type of house and area extremely well. It was where we wanted to be, and we knew before we even walked in that we would love it.

🏠 **Good news story**

I am a single first-time buyer and I went sale-agreed in June 2020 on a house that a receiver was selling, having been the successful bidder against 14 others. The problems soon ensued after that; one being that the house did not come with a certificate to state it was built in compliance with building regulations. The

---

receiver refused to pay for it and I had to pay €1,000 for something that is ordinarily supplied by the vendor, in order to be able to draw down on my mortgage. Contracts were exchanged in Oct 2020 and it was then discovered that the title deeds weren't correct, resulting in me waiting 2.5 years until this legal issue was resolved. After multiple complaints, countless discussions with various government departments and TDs, and four full mortgage approval offers later, I am due to get the keys of my forever home in a few short weeks!

Eimear, Wexford

The following is a checklist of questions that you can ask an estate agent when you go to a viewing and some things to look out for. Most agents won't be able (or willing) to answer all of these questions, but I believe it's good to be thorough and there is no harm in making them work for their money. Some of the questions you'll be able to figure out the answers to yourself by using the research steps listed in Chapter 8.

GENERAL QUESTIONS

- What's included in the price? Curtains, carpets, cooker, other appliances, lights?

- How flexible is the seller on the asking price?

- How long has the property been on the market?

- Why is the seller selling? Are they keen on a quick sale?

- Is the home subject to probate? If so, has it been lodged yet?

- Has there been much interest in the property, or any offers?

- What is the energy rating?

- What aspect is the garden or balcony?

- When was it built? (This could be important for home insurance, for example it is often difficult to get home insurance on a home that is over 100 years old and may require a specialist insurer.)

- Are there any other similar properties for sale in the area, and what are their asking prices?

- Has the property been altered in any way? (Certain alterations, such as a large area of flat roof, may cause issues with insurers.)

- How is the property heated? Is it insulated?

- Has there ever been a fire in the property?

- Has the property or local area ever flooded? (Again, this could be important for home insurance.)

- What kind of parking is available? (Think long-term. Will you ever need to charge an electric vehicle, or get a child in and out of a car?)

- Has there ever been any difficulty securing home (building and contents) insurance at normal rates?

- Are there any proposed developments in the area?

- How good is the WiFi in the area?

- What are the neighbours like? (Most agents won't admit if there are troublesome neighbours.)

- Has the roof been repaired or replaced since the property was built? (Applicable to houses only.)

- Is the property freehold or leasehold? (Applicable to houses only.)

- What level of snagging is included? (Applicable to new homes.)

- How old is the water boiler or water cylinder? When was it last serviced? If it was recently serviced, were there any follow-up repairs done?

- What is the annual service charge? (Applicable to apartments and multi-unit developments.)
- What schools and transport links are available? (Google Maps should get you this information but local knowledge can be useful for schools.)

THINGS TO LOOK OUT FOR

- How much have similar properties in the area sold for over the last few years? Use the property price register.
- Is the property in a potential flood zone? Check floodinfo.ie.
- How much will renovations cost?
- Does the boundary in the sales material match the one on the land registry?
- If they are part of the sale, do the appliances work? Do the windows open? Your surveyor should check these, along with taps, showers, toilets, but it's good to check yourself.

Again, it is worth remembering most estate agents will

not be able or willing to answer all of these questions. Also, the list is not exhaustive, but the answers will give you a good indication when deciding if this home is the right one for you. I would advise bringing a notebook with you to viewings and taking notes as you will often forget the answers to the above questions, especially if viewing multiple homes in the same day.

ACTION STEPS

- Print the list of questions or have it on your phone.
- Bring a notepad to make notes.

11

HOME RENOVATION COSTS AND TIPS

RENOVATIONS can vary greatly in cost depending on various factors such as the level of finish desired, type and location of home, and access to materials and labour.

It is generally more expensive to outsource all renovation work, but doing some tasks oneself can save money.

There may be benefits to renovating a home, as if you get a better BER rating you may be able to avail of a 'green rate' mortgage, which usually has a lower interest rate.

I often get asked how much renovations cost, especially since we did a full renovation ourselves, and I always give the same reply: 'It depends.' It's an overused answer but unfortunately, I can't be any more accurate than that without engaging the services of a quantity surveyor. Material and labour costs fluctuate and prices vary massively depending on the level of finish required, the type of home being renovated, location, access, and many other factors. I do, however, have rough guidelines which I will run through in this chapter.

If looking to outsource the work entirely, it is obviously going to cost a lot more than if you take on some of the work yourself. And, if you're doing a full renovation, there may be a lot more you can do yourself than you would think, especially if you have time and energy. For example, I ripped out a lot of our house by myself. It took me two months to do, but it cost me nothing (other than the price of lunch for some friends generous with their time and labour). I estimate that I saved around €5,000 by doing this myself. There's also a real sense of achievement in getting your hands dirty. I feel very proud sitting in our home now knowing that I had a hand in making it what it is.

If you're in any way handy, you can also do some of the construction works yourself. In 2022 RTÉ launched a show called *Build Your Own Home* and I thought it was fantastic. I love my Dermot Bannon and Hugh Wallace 'property porn' shows but let's be honest, the budgets in them are often far beyond what most people can afford. *Build Your Own Home* is far more realistic and gives a good insight into what you can actually do by yourself if you're motivated.

OUR PROJECT

Our renovation took about 12 months to complete. We started off doing some of the initial work ourselves, and then enlisted the help of friends in the trades for the building work. We also hired a retrofit company to handle the plumbing and to assist with obtaining grants from the Sustainable Energy Authority of Ireland (SEAI). Our goal was to improve the energy efficiency of our home, which was originally rated G on the Building Energy Rating (BER) scale (with A1 being the most efficient and G being the least efficient). We were able to upgrade the house to an A3 rating.

Works we did ourselves
- Cleared out the contents of the house
- Removed old carpets and fitted furniture
- Ripped out the old kitchen
- Removed the old bathroom. It was a retro pink bathroom that was back in style, but not to our taste. We listed it

for free on adverts.ie and someone came to take it for reuse in their own home.

- Tore down all of the ceilings. We needed to rewire and replumb the house and didn't like the stippled ceiling look.
- Tore down walls and removed the downstairs bathroom. This became our new kitchen.
- Removed all of the old wiring, after disconnecting the electricity.

Works done by the electrician, builder, and retrofit company

- Full rewiring
- New windows and doors
- New kitchen (including blocking up the old back door)
- New bathroom upstairs
- New toilet installed downstairs. This required digging a trench through the house to connect to the old waste pipe.
- Removal of internal supporting wall and installation of steel supports. This opened up the old kitchen and

living room to create one big room.

- Removal of window and creation of a new opening for French doors leading to the back garden
- Insulation of all external walls
- Full replumbing
- Installation of an air-to-water heat pump
- Installation of PV solar panels
- Pouring of concrete screed downstairs to level the floors
- Insulation of the attic with added flooring for extra storage.

And more. Essentially, we gutted the house down to the bricks and rebuilt it. The only thing we didn't do was get a new roof, which we will have to do soon. It was a gruelling (and costly) year of hard work but we made it to the end and now have a warm and energy-efficient home that feels like a new-build, even though it's 100 years old. The renovation cost us around €1,100 per square metre, but we received favourable rates from friends in the trades and some discounts through my Instagram page, so that figure is relatively low. That also includes savings by getting the SEAI grants. By upgrading the house to an A3 BER rating, we were able to switch to a 'green rate' mortgage with a fixed rate of 2.1 per cent for four years.

That's a brief summary of what we did. I could probably write a whole book about the renovation itself, but that's beyond the scope of this discussion. I just wanted to give you an idea of the process involved.

Renovation cost guidelines	
Renovations to existing building	€1,000 – €2,000 per square metre
Extension	€2,000 – €4,000 per square metre
Kitchen	€8,000 upwards
Bathroom	€8,000 – €12,000
Attic conversion	€15,000 – €25,000

These figures may be on the lower side or the generous side depending on the cost of materials at the time you're enquiring and they can also vary depending on where you are in the country. It is really difficult to gauge but I would recommend getting as many quotes as you can from builders, at least three anyway.

We learned a lot from doing our renovation. Here are

some of my top tips, along with some sent in by followers of my Instagram page.

⌇ Renovation Top tips

- The obvious first tip is to make a budget and stick to it. Keep a contingency in there for unexpected costs. 10 per cent is a frequently recommended number to have set aside for this.

- Use tradespeople and builders that have come highly recommended by friends or people you know that have actually employed them.

- Set up an estimates, quotes, costs and payments spreadsheet on Google Sheets. It's handy to have it on a cloud service like Google Sheets rather than an Excel spreadsheet so that it can be edited from any device, anywhere. It is vital you keep track of every euro spent, in the event of any queries about invoices or overspends.

- Be very clear with your instructions and expectations, and confirm everything before ordering. For example, we wanted a specific type of window, however upon delivery a different style of window arrived. The mistake was down to a miscommunication and my fault for not making sure the windows they were ordering for us were the exact ones we wanted. We were under pressure to order them before prices went up by 10 per cent so we put the order in before receiving an exact picture of what the windows would look like. The windows worked out ok in the end, but I still would have preferred the style we wanted originally.

- Leave a lot of room in your budget for skips, you will need more than you think.

- Using a lockbox is handy for when you have multiple people coming and going. Make sure you invest in a good-quality, secure lockbox.

- Plan for your renovation to take longer than expected or promised. There are always delays and things will happen outside of your control that will extend timelines. You may need to factor in additional costs for accommodation if you need to rent elsewhere while renovating.

- Expect the unexpected, especially if it is an old house. I've watched enough renovation shows to know that all houses have unexpected surprises that can only be uncovered when you start the work. Nobody plans for woodworm in the attic joists, subsidence or structural cracks, but they happen.

- If the property needs to be rewired, the walls may need to be 'chased' (have channels cut into them to hold the cables). Some electricians may do this themselves, while others may require it to be done before they begin their work. You may need to do it yourself or pay your builder to do it. It can be a messy job and is best done early on in the renovation process.

- Make out a clear outline of the order in which things should be done. Your builder will help with this and it will depend on what works are being done. For example, you want to ensure there is a working toilet at all times and so may need to hire a portaloo. You might find that works in one room impact those in another (especially where plumbing and wiring are involved), so have a clear vision for the whole house and prepare a schedule of works listing the order of jobs.

- If you're working on a period property, you will have to make sure there are no restrictions on what you can do. If it is a listed building, you will be limited in what you can do and how much you can change. You should also talk to a professional about any additional planning requirements that may be necessary.

- You will need a specific type of insurance for a home that is vacant while being renovated. Talk to your home insurer and make sure you are covered while works are ongoing.

- Think about future-proofing your house. At the beginning of our renovation, we planned on simply installing a combi-boiler, but eventually decided to opt for a heat pump as we wanted to future-proof the house as much as possible while we had the chance. We wanted to avoid more renovation works down the line.

- You can never have too many sockets. Print out a floor plan and sit down with your electrician and discuss where you will need sockets, lights and switches in relation to where furniture will go. We opted for most of our sockets to have built-in USB ports which are handy, especially behind a TV. We also installed sockets that have built-in WiFi boosters. You could do a drawing for each room and stick them on the wall so the electrician is reminded often.

- Use zip-up door covers to stop dust going from one room into another.

- Document everything with as many photos and videos as you can. It's great being able to look back through all of the videos and photos we took to show us just how much work was done on our house. Everyone loves a good 'before and after'!

- You will likely be making many trips to the builders' suppliers. It could be a good idea to set up a trade account and you may get a reduction in delivery charges.

- Make a list of works to be done in each room and check it off as you go along. It is easy to become overwhelmed by the size of the overall task, especially if you are doing a lot of the work yourself. A list will help keep things moving along.

- It is best to put money into the basics like rewiring, plumbing and insulation. Although these things can't be seen, they are not the areas to do on the cheap. If money is tight, it is most important to get the bones of the renovation done well. Later, you can try to save money by buying used appliances and furniture. These can be replaced easily, insulation cannot.

- Be patient. The process is stressful and making decisions can be difficult, and the stress can be taken out on partners or spouses. Be kind to each other and remember that it will all be worth it in the end.

- You probably won't get everything you want done. Some things linger for months and years after moving in. It's best to accept this from the beginning, some things will never be finished!

- Install a light and sockets in the attic.

- Install sockets, lights and a tap outside.

- Think about spending a little extra on the finishes of your electrics. For example; you will need isolation switches in the kitchen for each appliance. We got all of ours onto one plate and had the metal switches engraved with the name of each appliance. It was about €100 extra but looks really good compared to the standard white plastic switches with a sticker underneath them.

- Some decisions are going to take a lot longer than you think. There are far more tiles to choose from than you would have ever imagined.

- Think about delivery times and make sure items are ordered early. Some things can take months to be delivered and you don't want those items holding everything else up.

- Insulate everywhere you can. You won't regret it. If you're pulling down the ceilings, take the opportunity to insulate between floors with acoustic insulation which will limit the transfer of noise between floors. This is one of the best decisions we made as it means the house is quiet and you cannot hear the downstairs TV when you're upstairs. Especially helpful if you plan on having or have young children.

- If you have the facility to move out, I would recommend

it. It's tough living on a building site.

- Lots of people recommend living in the home before renovating, as it helps to know where the light falls and where you like to spend most of your time. This wasn't something we could do, but I know others found it really helpful to live in the home first.

- It is worth making the effort to improve the BER of the home to a B3 or higher as this means you can qualify for the lower 'green rate' from most mortgage providers.

- Clearly outline your expectations in a document, share with the builder and have agreed sign-off.

🏠 **Good news story**

I am a single, first-time buyer, but also a legally-separated, single parent. I saved for three years to get the deposit together to get outbid left, right and centre! At the start of house hunting, I wrote a wish list: a house close to my family (not too close), a utility, a playroom for my daughter (to keep the toys confined), and a real fire. After two years house hunting,

---

I was starting to compromise on all that just to get us a place of our own. Then a house that had gone sale-agreed well out of my price range came up again and I bid the asking, which was slightly above my budget, and I crossed my fingers. Well, I'm currently on my sofa in that house and it has everything on my wish list. Your good news stories are what kept me going. I really believe everything happens for a reason.

Aileen, Cork

So, if you're looking at a home and it needs a lot of work, don't be put off. Even in today's market, there is still value in a 'fixer-upper' if you go about it the right way. There is also the added benefit of the home being custom-made to your own preferences. My advice would be to get a really good idea of the full costs of the home plus the renovation and gauge whether it is a good-value purchase by using nearby comparisons.

Make sure that the home's value increases by at least as much as you need to spend on your renovation, but ideally by a lot more so that you can have equity in your home after all that hard work. Ideally, you could increase the home's value and this would then mean you could look to switch your mortgage to a better rate by either using a lower LTV (loan to value) or a green rate. This could reduce your mortgage payment by thousands a year.

ACTION STEPS

- Before starting a renovation, it is important to research the extent of the work needed and to consult with a quantity surveyor or builder to get a rough estimate of the cost.
- It is important to have a plan for funding the renovation and to consider where you will live during the construction process, if necessary.

12

ADDITIONAL COSTS WHEN BUYING A HOME

THIS chapter explains the additional costs to consider when buying a home in Ireland, including: stamp duty, solicitor's fees, land registry fees, valuer's report, surveyor's fees, property tax, home insurance, mortgage protection insurance, and moving costs.

Hopefully, if you've read this far, you'll have your deposit (10 per cent of the purchase price) saved and are looking to move on to the next step. Getting that deposit together is not easy, and unfortunately the job is not over when you do have it as there are quite a few other costs associated with buying a home in Ireland. In this chapter I will outline those extra costs and give you a rough idea of how much they will be.

Before a bank can evaluate your mortgage application, there are other significant expenses that you will need to save for. You will have to show your lender that you have saved enough to cover all or most of the costs listed below. The following list excludes any renovation costs and focuses on the basics.

⌗→ Top tip

As mentioned at the beginning of the book, when saving up your deposit, try and aim for 12 per cent or 13 per cent to cover the additional costs outlined in this chapter.

Further costs at a glance

Stamp duty	1 per cent of purchase price up to €1 million. 2 per cent of anything in excess of €1 million.
Solicitor's fees	€1,200 – €2,000 plus VAT (professional fees)
Land registry fees (usually added to solicitor's fees)	Around €1,000
Folio and search fees (usually added to solicitor's fees)	Around €250
Valuer's report	€150 – €200
Surveyor's fees (or snag list)	€450 – €700 including VAT
Property tax	Depends on valuation band, usually between €300 and €700 per year
Home insurance	Usually under €500 per year
Mortgage protection insurance	Around €20 – €50 per month
Management fees (for apartments and some homes)	Varying
Alarm installation	Varying
Moving costs	Around €1,200

STAMP DUTY

Stamp duty will probably be the single biggest extra cost you need to consider. For most, it is 1 per cent of the purchase price. So, for example, if you are buying a home for €300,000, you will need €30,000 deposit and €3,000 for stamp duty. If the value of the home is over €1,000,000, stamp duty is 1 per cent for the first million and then 2 per cent of anything over that. If you are buying a new-build, it is 1 per cent of the price excluding VAT (13.5 per cent).

Example

You buy a new-build for €400,000. Your stamp duty will be 1 per cent of €346,000 as that is the price excluding VAT. So, instead of paying €4,000 stamp duty, you will pay €3,460.

SOLICITOR AND SEARCH FEES

Your solicitor will have a 'professional fee' as well as other fees. Solicitors usually include the cost of your stamp duty in their fees. Here are our exact solicitor's fees for our home purchase. I have removed our stamp duty.

Professional fees (excluding VAT)	€1,200
Paper, postage, etc.	€50
VAT @ 23%	€287.50
Total	€1,537.50

Outlays not subject to VAT:

Land registry fee on deed of transfer	€800.00
Land registry fee on mortgage deed	€175.00
Folio and filed plan	€40.00
Search fees	€200
Total outlays	€1,215.00
Total costs (excluding stamp duty)	€2,752.50

VALUER'S REPORT

Your lender will require a valuation on the home you have agreed to buy to assess whether or not it is worth the price you're paying (the amount they are lending on it). The lender will give you a list of valuers they use, and you book it yourself and pay them directly. In my opinion, this system is ridiculous as most 'valuers' are estate agents, so it is in their interest to value the home as high as possible; a rising tide lifts all boats. I have heard stories of valuers not even going into the home to assess it, simply calling the person and asking what price they're paying and putting that down on the valuation. For the last few years, a lot of homes have been selling for way above their asking price, yet I have rarely heard of a valuer saying the sale-agreed price was too high. Most of the time, they will value it at whatever you are willing to pay. Time will tell if this practice will come back to haunt lenders, but either way the service will cost you around €200.

🏠 Good news story

Nearly two years trying to buy. Had such bad luck with properties and estate agents. Finally, found an honest estate agent and an honest seller. Went sale agreed and drawing down shortly. The owner refused a counter bid from an investor which was such a humble thing to do. She wanted the house to be lived in by a family. She even asked to meet us and she was so lovely. Cannot wait to finally be in our first home. The seller lives next door. I can see us being friends in the future.

Jenna, Tipperary

SURVEYOR'S FEES

When you're buying a home, it will either require a pre-purchase survey (existing home) or a snag list (new-build). It is important that the surveyor you use for this task is registered, qualified and insured with the relevant authorities.

The survey will look at the following:

- Visible defects and potential problems caused by hidden issues
- Potential repair options needed
- Visual inspection of all accessible parts of the property
- Assessment of all major and minor faults: taps working, toilets flushing, window openings, and so on
- Condition of the heating system
- Investigation of damp levels and insulation
- Information on environmental hazards like asbestos. The survey will not test for asbestos, but will say if asbestos is likely to be present.
- Any other potential issues like trees nearby that may cause damage if they fall.

It is very important that you read the survey once it is completed and talk to a professional about what might be necessary to fix and what is not a cause for concern. This survey is then sent to the lender so they can make sure that the home is habitable. If there are any major issues, the property may require a structural survey or a more in-depth inspection of areas not visible without invasive measures like removing wallpaper or plaster. From my experience, the results of surveys can sound alarming. I believe this is just so the surveyor can cover their backs in the event of a legal issue, so they flag a lot of things as 'potentially a problem' and 'advise further inspection'. However, more often than not, there is nothing to worry about. Even if the sale doesn't go through, you will have to pay for the surveyor.

PROPERTY TAX

This is a self-assessed tax that you must pay each year. You pay it through Revenue online. There is an interactive tool on revenue.ie where you input your eircode and it brings up a map with a suggested value of your home.

From this, you can either pay for the year in advance or via equal instalments throughout the year. So, on the revenue.ie website you go to 'calculate your local property tax' (LPT) and then select the applicable criteria from the dropdown menus. The total amount of LPT due (including any local authority rate adjustment) for your property will be displayed.

HOME INSURANCE

Home insurance is a type of insurance that covers your home, its contents, and personal belongings from various risks such as fire, theft, and water damage. It may also cover damage to surrounding structures, like fences and garages, and provide liability coverage for injuries that occur on your property. Home insurance policies may include buildings insurance, which covers the physical structure of your home, contents insurance, which covers your personal belongings, all-risks cover for valuables, and liability insurance. You can purchase home insurance directly from insurance companies or use comparison websites or brokers to find the best policy for you. It is

ADDITIONAL COSTS WHEN BUYING A HOME

important to carefully review the terms and coverage of a policy before purchasing to ensure that it meets your needs. I recommend going to ccpc.ie and looking at their very thorough advice on home insurance.

You should estimate your insurance to cost around €400 to €500 per year.

MORTGAGE PROTECTION

See Chapter 6.

MANAGEMENT FEES

Most apartments and some housing estates will require a monthly or annual management fee. This is to look after the buildings, grounds, elevators, and any other on-site upkeep required. Often, if buying an apartment, you will have to pay the previous owner back some of their management fees 'pro-rata'. Basically, you are responsible for the fees from when you take over the property. You may need to pay these fees up front, so if you buy an apartment in January, you might have to pay management fees for the year. It is worth keeping in mind.

ALARM INSTALLATION

If the home you are buying already has an alarm system, then you should be ok. However, if it does not, you may need to budget for having an alarm installed. These can vary from very expensive to relatively cheap. It depends on the system and whether it is monitored professionally or self-monitored.

MOVING FEES

Moving in Ireland can be expensive, with costs including hiring a moving company, renting a truck or van, fuel, packing materials, and additional services such as packing and unpacking. Hiring a moving company may cost around €500 for a local move with a one-bedroom apartment and €2,000 for a long-distance move with a four-bedroom house. Renting a truck or van can cost €50 to €100 per day. Fuel costs will depend on distance and vehicle efficiency, with a long-distance move in a large truck costing around €200 and a local move in a small van costing closer to €50. Packing materials, including boxes, tape, bubble wrap and padding, may cost around €100 for a one-bedroom apartment and €300 for a four-bedroom house. Professional packing and unpacking services may cost €500 for a one-bedroom apartment and €1,000 for a four-bedroom house. It is important to get quotes from multiple moving companies and consider your budget and needs when deciding on the best option.

ACTION STEPS

- Do your research on home insurance and mortgage protection and get an idea of how much they will cost you.

13

TIPS FOR THE BIDDING PROCESS

- This chapter will arm you with the knowledge on how to bid and how much to bid.
- Revisit Chapter 9 to prepare for bidding.

THIS is going to be an extremely important chapter for you, especially if bidding wars are still a thing whenever you're reading this book. The tips in here have been gathered from conversations with thousands of people who have been successful with their bidding and also from multiple estate agents who very kindly gave me some inside knowledge. We never actually won a bidding war; all of our efforts were unsuccessful because we refused to pay more than what we felt the home was worth. However, I did have two agents come back to me to accept a previous offer but by then we had moved on.

There was one house in Rialto we liked and we offered

€25,000 below the asking price as, from my research, I felt it was overpriced. Within minutes, we were outbid. I wasn't willing to go any higher and we let the house go. Six weeks later, the agent emailed to say the sale had fallen through and the vendor was willing to accept our original offer if we were still interested. Thankfully, by then we had found our home. I recently checked how much it sold for – exactly what we had offered. I love when I'm right.

This happens a lot. It worked out well for us in the end, but I must emphasise that this could be the most stressful, anger-inducing stage of your home-buying journey. The process here in Ireland is archaic; you get more transparency buying a piece of steak here than you do buying your home. You never know for sure who you are bidding against or how the estate agent is going to treat you. It is a brutal process and I would love to see changes made to make it more transparent, simple and time-effective, but more on that later.

BEFORE BIDDING

Chapter 8 is vital for this. Make sure your research is

done on the property and on the area. Know what sold recently and how much for. Use this research and your own circumstances to set a maximum bid in advance and stick to it. If the home needs work, have a rough idea of renovation costs and factor them into your bid. Your max bid is very important, do whatever you can to avoid being caught up in a bidding war.

🔑 Top tip

It is worth remembering here that if you are approved for a regular mortgage (not a renovation mortgage as described in Chapter 4), your mortgage approval will usually be based on a 'loan to value' (LTV) of 90 per cent. If you manage to buy a home for less than your maximum mortgage approval, unfortunately you do not have extra money for furniture, new windows or redecorating.

For example; let's say you're a first-time buyer (FTB) with €30,000 saved and you have mortgage approval for €240,000. Your maximum spend is €270,000.

If you manage to find a home for €250,000, this does

not mean your lender will give you the full €240,000 and you only have to add €10,000, leaving you with €20,000 extra for works. Your lender will only lend a maximum of 90 per cent on this, so you will still need a 10 per cent deposit (€25,000 in this case) and your lender will provide the remainder (€225,000). This is something I come across a lot. People sometimes think that their maximum mortgage approval is what they will get, but it is the LTV that is most important.

DURING BIDDING

Always email your bid so that you have a record of it in writing. Some agents use online bidding platforms and some don't. Whatever medium the agent uses, they will require proof of funds from you. This is a good thing as it means the agents are ensuring that there are no time-wasters bidding on the property who could drive up the price unnecessarily.

Now comes the tricky part: do you send them your full 'approval in principle' (AIP) amount? Or do you redact the figures? This is one I always struggle with. While I understand agents need to be sure people have the funds to back up their bids, I do not think it is a good idea for the agent to know exactly how much you have to spend. If they know you have approval to go to a higher number, you can be sure they will do whatever they can to get it out of you. Their job, at the end of the day, is to get the highest price they can for the vendor. I always recommend that you send your AIP with the figures redacted. Most agents will accept this as it shows you have approval. Most people are not time-wasters, they have no interest in bidding on houses they cannot afford.

If the agent does not accept the redacted AIP, you could ask your lender or broker or solicitor to send an email to confirm you have the funds to back up your offer. Again, this may not be enough for some agents and you will just have to make the decision yourself whether or not you think it is a good idea to send them your unredacted approval amount.

With that said, it is a good idea to build a rapport with estate agents in your area. Show them you are serious about buying your home and that you are organised and ready to move quickly. Agents prefer a sale that is more likely to go through, which does not always mean the highest bid, but the best offer. Your bid is just the money, your offer is the whole package: your situation, your organisation, your ability to buy immediately with funds approved, your solicitor in place, that you are not in a chain, and so on. If an agent has two offers in and around the same amount, they will advise the vendor which offer they feel should be accepted and that will usually be the one that is most likely to follow through. The last thing an agent wants is a sale falling through as it delays everything, including their commission.

If you've built up a rapport with an estate agent, they will know your situation and circumstances. If you have put in an offer, you could ask that the agent inform the vendor about your situation and the positives you bring to the deal: you'll be an owner-occupier who loves the home and area, the house will become a family home, and any other factors that may convince them that you are the safest bet. Make a fair first offer based on your research. I would always advise that you start below asking price and work from there, but don't put in an insulting offer that's too low. That can irritate the vendor and the agent. You want to show them both that you are ready for a quick and smooth buying process, with no risk of it falling through.

🏘 Good news story

After 13 years in Dublin, I sold my house and moved my new baby home to Mayo. I thought I would have no problem buying a house but with the surge in prices and demand for houses after Covid, I was constantly outbid by thousands and as a solo parent it started to feel impossible. Followed crazy house prices and loved the idea of the letters to houses so I contacted the vendor of one property that I thought was my dream home but it wasn't to be. I was once again outbid. I really thought I'd never find a home for my son and I. Amazingly, after two years searching I picked up the keys to our new-build home and I couldn't be happier! We're one of the lucky ones and I'll be forever grateful as sadly it's not the same outcome for everyone.

Edel, Mayo

YOUR BUYING POSITION

Your buying position can dictate your buying strength and how to bid. If there are other bidders, you can ask the agent about their buying positions. Most agents will let you know what type of other bidders are involved. Armed with this information, you can then determine how they rank against you in terms of buying strength.

Cash buyer

The strongest competition you can have. A lot of the time, these are investors. They are strong because they are not relying on third parties like banks or insurance companies. They can buy quickly and easily. Even if a cash buyer offers less than you, it is possible their bid will be accepted over yours.

Mortgage buyer

The bidder has mortgage approval, is ready to buy and is not waiting on the sale of their own property.

HOW TO BUY A HOME IN IRELAND

Chain buyer

This bidder is likely to be considered a 'weak' bidder if the sale of their own property is in its early stages. If it is at an advanced stage, then they may be considered as strong as the mortgage buyer.

BIDDING STRATEGY

Depending on your buying position, you may need to bid more, less or just match another bidder. For example, if you are a mortgage buyer and are bidding against a chain buyer, you may be able to just match their bid as you will be considered in a stronger buying position. However, if you are a mortgage buyer and are bidding against a cash buyer, then you may have to bid more as your buying position is weaker than theirs. As I said, it is not always the highest bid that wins but the best offer. Use your own judgement and bid however you see appropriate, but remember to stick to your original maximum bid amount that you identified.

MATCHING A BID

This is always a difficult one. If you do want to match a bid, you need to show why your offer is better than the current one (i.e. your buying position). A lot of agents will say they cannot accept your bid if you just match whatever the current highest bid is and that you must increase your bid. However, legally, estate agents must present all offers to the vendor. A lot of agents do not like matching bids as it brings an end to the bidding war.

The problem is this: agents have a lot of power when it comes to offers and advising the vendor on which offer to accept. Matching a bid may anger the agent and they may purposely advise the vendor to accept the other offer. So, it is a good idea to word your offer well, be fair and polite, explain why you are matching the bid and not exceeding the existing bid. Highlight the benefits of your offer over the other bidder: that you're organised, more likely to follow through, and so on. It could be a useful tactic if the bidding war has brought the bids on a house up much higher than the asking price, but not something I would advise if the house is at or below asking price.

INCREMENTS

There is no proven strategy when it comes to how much to increase your bid by and it will depend on the home, its asking price and whether the bidding is done online or via the estate agent. It is always a good idea to think about your increases as a percentage of the overall price. For example, a €500 increase on a bid of €650,000 is a much smaller percentage increase than €500 on a bid of €200,000. You could aim for a percentage of the bid, for example increasing your bid by 0.25 per cent each time.

0.25 per cent of €650,000 is 650,000 x 0.0025 = €1,625

0.25 per cent of €200,000 is 200,000 x 0.0025 = €500

Sometimes, if you are the only party bidding on a home but the vendor or estate agent has a number in mind they want to achieve (and yours is below), they may ask you to increase your offer to get close to or equal the figure they want. Personally, I would never bid against myself but, as above, this is just going to have to be a personal judgement call and whether or not you feel the home is worth it.

Best and final offers

Sometimes, when a bidding war has escalated and the bids are all far in excess of the asking price, the estate agent will ask all bidders for their 'best and final offer'. This is done to try and bring a halt to the bids and get towards an agreed sale price. This is a blind bid: you do not know what the others are going to offer and must go with your own head and offer what you feel the home is worth to you. Most of the time, this will go to whoever bids the highest amount but, as stated earlier, it is not always about the highest bid but the best offer. The decision is at the discretion of the agent and the vendor.

In recent times, there has been a small movement of sellers who have refused to sell to investors or investment funds, and opted instead to sell to an owner-occupier despite their bid being a little lower. Personally, I would love to see more of this; however, investors will often offer the highest amount, so it is very difficult for vendors to reject extra cash. Remember that the estate agent has a great influence on which offer is accepted, so use the good rapport you have built with them and the strategies above to give yourself the best chance of being successful. Good luck!

ACTION STEPS

- Research the property and area to determine its value.
- Set a maximum bid in advance, taking into account any renovation costs.
- Be aware of your mortgage approval amount and the loan-to-value (LTV) ratio.
- Have proof of funds ready to provide to the agent.

14

SALE-AGREED:
WHAT HAPPENS NEXT?

- This chapter will inform you of what needs to be done next and who is responsible.
- You will learn about potential issues that may arise and how to navigate them.

YOU have found the ideal home, your bid has been accepted, the mortgage has been set up, and there it is in black and white: a confirmation that the sale has been agreed upon. You would think that this is it, but unfortunately, you're not quite there yet.

Going 'sale-agreed' is just one of the steps in what is a very lengthy and complicated journey towards owning your own home. In this chapter I will outline exactly what 'sale-agreed' means and what happens next. You're nearly there.

Does 'sale-agreed' mean the deal is done?

In Ireland, sale-agreed basically means an agreement by the two parties to the purchase/sale of the home. Think of it like a handshake. It's a non-binding agreement. Nothing is certain until both parties sign the contracts, so there are some legal and surveying steps still to be done to make sure everything is ok. Until the contracts are signed, the vendor or the buyer can pull out of the agreement at any stage, for any reason. This means being sale-agreed can be a stressful and sometimes lengthy wait.

There are a number of factors that can delay a sale and sometimes the process can drag on so long that the buyer or vendor will withdraw from the agreement. The home might be tied up in probate (property owned by a deceased person that is being sold), which I have seen take anywhere from fourteen weeks to three years. Or a structural problem with the home may arise during the survey forcing the buyer to withdraw. Or house prices may have increased significantly since going 'sale-agreed' and the vendor wants to put the home back on the market to get more money. I have seen this happen far too many times over the last two years.

You could get a surprise in the pre-purchase survey and the home may require more work than initially expected, resulting in unexpected expenses. A common question I am asked is: can I renegotiate the price? You absolutely can, but it will depend on the level of works required and some other factors. The vendor is entitled to refuse to lower the price and go to the next highest bidder or go back to the market. I have heard of people getting tens of thousands knocked off the sale-agreed price after negotiation, but it depends on the home and the level of demand for it. Someone else may be willing to pay the same price and absorb the fixing costs themselves. So, this one is up to you.

Let's put our positive hats on for a moment and assume that everything is fine and the sale will go through, which is more often the case than not. Here is a checklist of what happens next and who is responsible for organising.

- Solicitor notified that you have gone sale-agreed (you)
- Booking deposit paid to the estate agent (you and solicitor)
- Pre-purchase survey (you)

- Agree on what is to be included in the sale (you and vendor/estate agent)
- Lender's valuer organised (you)
- Mortgage protection (you)
- Home insurance (you)
- Submit final documents to your lender: most recent payslips, and anything else they may require (you)
- Review surveyor's report and get quotes for fixing if necessary (you)
- Give notice to existing landlord (you: if currently renting, but be careful with this as the sale can still fall through and you do not want to be left with nowhere to live)
- Transfer of funds to solicitor (you, your lender and solicitor)
- Solicitor completes final legal checks (solicitor)
- Final walkthrough of the home before collecting the keys (you and estate agent)
- Funds transferred (solicitor)
- Collect keys and buy champagne!

Notify solicitor

The first thing you need to do is inform your solicitor and pay your booking deposit: usually around €5 – 10,000 depending on the sale. This is refundable if anything goes wrong or you change your mind.

Organise your surveyor (see Chapter 12)

A standard 'pre-purchase survey' should be fine for most homes. If it's more complex, you may need a structural engineer. This will cost you around €450 – €700 including VAT.

Agree on what is to be included

I have seen cases of vendors removing flooring and even kitchens after going sale-agreed, so make sure you get *in writing* exactly what is included in the sale: light fittings, furniture, white goods, curtains and carpets, and so on.

Organise the valuer

The bank or lender will usually give you a list of valuers they use and you organise this yourself with the valuer and the estate agent.

Get your mortgage protection sorted

You do not have to go with your lender's policy here, despite what they tell you (see Chapter 6) but mortgage protection is essential to have in place before you can draw down your mortgage. So, make sure to set it up well in advance. Remember, you can delay the policy's start date and only pay when it starts.

Home insurance

Make sure to shop around for home insurance. If you are renovating and the home will be vacant, be sure to confirm this with your insurer as it requires a different type of home insurance. We got a standard home insurance policy to draw down, but once we started renovations we switched to a policy called 'home under construction' which allows the home to be vacant. It covers the building, not contents.

Submit final documents

Your lender may require your most recent payslips to ensure your employment conditions have not changed since going sale-agreed. They will also require a copy of the sur-

SALE-AGREED: WHAT HAPPENS NEXT?

vey and usually the valuer sends their report directly to the lender.

Surveyor's report

These reports are often lengthy and detailed, but also vague. You must make sure to read it properly. The survey only looks at what is visible, and is not invasive. This means they will often include a lot of 'possible' issues with the home. If there are any major issues, the survey will show these and highlight if they require fixing to allow draw-down. Your lender will let you know. This can potentially lead to a delay and possibly the sale falling through.

Transfer of funds

Once everything goes well and there are no issues, your solicitor will request the funds from the lender and hold the money in their account before transferring it to the vendors. Again, there is no definite timeline for this and it can often take weeks.

Final checks

While waiting on the funds, your solicitor will complete their final checks to make sure everything is still ok with the sale. This is also a good time to arrange a date for collecting the keys.

Final walkthrough

I recommend you organise a final walkthrough before funds are transferred to make sure that the home is left as agreed. If you negotiated for furniture or other items to be removed, this is your chance to make sure that this job has been done. It is always a good idea to check the attic and shed, if applicable, to make sure that they have been cleared out if this is what was agreed.

Collecting keys

When everything has been finalised and you have signed the last of the forms with your solicitor, it is now time to collect your keys and enjoy your new home.

🏠 Good news story

Myself and my partner were sale agreed on a house, it was the first house we weren't outbid on. The process went on for months, there were multiple issues coming up around planning permission, structural integrity, etc. Eventually the bank advised they couldn't lend on the house because they had a duty of care to us. We were devastated but I got back on the wagon the following day, applied for viewings and two weeks later we were sale agreed on our dream home! Your advice from your page was a big help and I emailed the estate agent after the viewing stating how much we loved the house and that we were willing to get the process started straight away. The process was like a dream for this house and we've now been living here for six months, preparing for our first Christmas in our home and have never been happier!

Amy, Dublin

HOW LONG WILL IT TAKE?

Unfortunately, there is no definite timeline for how long it takes to go from sale-agreed to keys in hand. It can take a long time, which is why it is important to have lots of the essentials organised beforehand, like your solicitor, mortgage protection, surveyor, and so on. Unfortunately, a lot of this is outside of your control and no matter how organised you are, some things will just take a long time. It is one of the biggest complaints I see in my inbox; people stressed and frustrated at how slow everything is going and how they feel like they have no idea what is happening, who is responsible for what and when things will be finished. Unfortunately, that's how it is in Ireland.

COMMON PROBLEMS

These are some of the most frequent questions and problems that I have encountered over the years. I wish I had more definite answers for you but the reality is you're just going to have to be patient and stay on top of things. A lot of the post-sale-agreed process is out of your hands.

Why does it take so long?

The three main parties involved when you go sale-agreed are solicitors, lenders and estate agents, and they will often blame each other for slowing things down.

At the moment, banks seem to be the main culprit due to a lack of qualified staff to deal with the large number of applications. Two banks have recently left the market (Ulster Bank and KBC) which has resulted in a lot of mortgage-switching applications on top of the usual drawdown volume and all this work is now going to a smaller pool of banks. This is not good news for anyone. It means competition is decreased, which reduces pressure on lenders to be competitive with their interest rates. They are also not properly staffed to handle the large volume of mortgage drawdown applications.

Probate

In Ireland, probate is the legal process of verifying a will and appointing an executor to manage a deceased person's assets, pay debts and taxes, and distribute remaining assets to beneficiaries. It may be required for property or significant assets and can be complex, especially for larger estates or disputes among beneficiaries. If the deceased person left a will, the person who deals with the estate is called the deceased person's executor. The executor needs to take out probate. The house cannot be sold until the grant of probate is issued. This is a problem here in Ireland as homes are often advertised for sale before the probate application has been lodged. Again, there is a lack of staff in the probate office, and they only accept applications from solicitors via post. I have seen the sale of certain estates in probate take years to complete. The average used to be around 16 weeks but it seems to be taking a lot longer now. The probate office takes around 14 weeks to review an application, after which they then raise any queries with the probate solicitor. Their response can go back to the end of the queue and take another 14 weeks. If there is a query or dispute to do with the distribution of the estate from a relative, the process can be pushed back to the end of the queue yet again. Another common problem I see is that estate agents or vendors claim that probate has been lodged when, in fact, it has not.

There is a website you can use to check if a probate has been granted. It is updated daily: http://probate.courts.ie/probate.nsf

There is something called a 'caretaker's agreement' that could be a potential solution in the case of a delayed probate. Here the buyer can essentially move in and there is an agreement between both parties. This is something that you should seek legal advice on.

Lack of communication

This is a very common frustration for buyers. They feel like there is a lack of communication after going sale-agreed, and that the solicitors, agents and lenders assume that the buyer knows what to do and how things will go.

Unfortunately, this is not the case and the sense of confusion on the buyer's behalf leads to feelings of frustration and stress. It would be beneficial for all parties involved to be more understanding of each other and communicate better what is going on and where the sale is at each step, but unfortunately that is not how things are done in Ireland. I have a suggestion in Chapter 14 that I believe could solve this problem. I think it is understandable for buyers to feel frustrated. I have been there, but the buyers are only dealing with one sale. The agents, solicitors and lenders are dealing with multiple sales at the same time. So, it requires patience and persistence. Thankfully, by reading this book, you'll be more informed and hopefully less stressed about the whole thing.

🏠 Good news story

My fiancé and I started to rent in May 2021, paying €1,950 for a two-bed apartment in Santry. We were there three months and realised we could never have a home if we stayed, so we made the difficult choice to move back to our parents' houses separately while basically sharing our daughter between houses. April 2022 went sale-agreed in the area we wanted and where our family was. Even though the house went €40,000 over asking it was still within budget and we were happy with it. Probate happened. Seven months later in November 2022 we got our forever home and we are now trying to make it a dream for us.

David, Dublin

ACTION STEPS

- Have your checklist and know who is responsible for which jobs.
- Keep on top of things and be as organised as you can to try and limit delays.
- Make sure you have, in writing, what is agreed to be left in the house and what is to be removed.
- Do a final walkthrough before transferring funds.

15

GOT THE KEYS? ADMIN AND MOVING IN CHECKLIST

- This chapter will run through what you need to do when moving into a new home.
- If you're renting, make sure you give the adequate notice period.
- There are steps you need to take to make sure everything is transferred in time, like internet, mail forwarding, etc.

YOU finally did it. Getting the keys to your first home is one of the best feelings in your life, and considering how difficult it is for this generation, it is something to be very proud of. The stress, the disappointment, the setbacks and the tears ... it's all worth it once you're settled into your own home. The jobs listed in this chapter will help make sure your transition to your new home is as organised as possible. Now would be a good time to learn your new eircode, as you're going to be using it a lot. Also, make sure you know the current alarm code if the home has an alarm system installed; you don't want your first time turning that key in the door to be ruined by the alarm going off for ages!

If you have been renting, you must provide the landlord with the necessary notice if you decide to vacate the property. Check your written lease or tenancy agreement to determine if a notice period has been specified. To prevent any disagreements with your landlord, you should carefully review the other terms of your contract. When giving your notice to depart, your landlord must abide by the conditions of any lease and the laws governing residential tenancies. The Residential Tenancies Board (RTB) and Threshold are the places to go to for advice on this.

Before you move out you should:

- Check the inventory
- Clean the accommodation
- Document the condition of the property, use photographs where possible
- Pay any outstanding bills or charges, otherwise you risk losing part or all of your deposit.

The rtb.ie website has more information on what happens at the end of a tenancy.

Transferring utilities

If you are moving from rented accommodation, your landlord may ask you to transfer these services into their name. Take final readings for all metered services before you leave, so that the utility companies can issue final bills, and ensure that you have paid any charges that you owe.

If the home you have bought was previously owned by someone else, you could ask them to change the utility accounts over to your name and to make sure there are no outstanding balances. In order to ensure that everything is set up for when you move in, get in touch with the utility providers as early as you can. As soon as you acquire control of the property, take the initial readings for all meter services. Document the readings with photos. Utility providers are well used to these switch-overs and will talk you through everything. It is not as much hassle as you might think. The majority of utility providers will give you instructions for moving or transferring your account on their websites, and you may even be able to do it all online yourself.

Transferring your telephone, broadband and TV services

Depending on where you are moving to and the coverage available, you may be able to transfer your account(s) from your former address for these services. Check with your service provider(s) to see if your account(s) may be transferred or if you will need to arrange for these services individually in your new home. In order for these services to be transferred when you move in, you should give your provider at least one month's notice. This could also be a good time to shop around for a better deal on these services, or to start up a new subscription with your present provider from your new address.

Transferring your TV licence

Now, obviously you are a law-abiding citizen and have paid your TV licence ... so this also needs to be transferred to your new address. You can do this online if you have your TV reference number and PIN. You can also do this in your local post office.

Redirecting your mail

An Post has a handy redirection service that you can set up online or in your local post office. This service is typically available for one, three, six, or twelve months. You will be required to give proof of your identity as well as proof of your previous address, as well as pay the relevant charge. An Post will then redirect all of your mail to your new address beginning on the agreed-upon date.

Places you may need to inform about your change of address:

- Electoral register (checktheregister.ie)
- Car insurance
- Driving licence (ndls.ie)
- Vehicle registration
- Home insurance
- Health insurance
- Life insurance
- Gadget insurance

- Schools and/or colleges
- Your bank
- Revenue.ie
- Your employer
- Your doctor.

Here is a checklist of things you might need to buy or bring with you to get you through your first week in your new home. I am assuming you know you will need beds, bedding and furniture:

- ○ Wine or champagne and glasses
- ○ Carbon monoxide/smoke/fire alarms
- ○ Fire blanket/extinguisher
- ○ Radiator valve key
- ○ New locks for doors
- ○ Rubbish bins and bin bags
- ○ Step ladder
- ○ Sweeping brush and mop
- ○ Toolbox, tools and measuring tape
- ○ Toilet roll, toilet brush and toilet cleaner
- ○ Window cleaner

- ○ Welcome mat
- ○ Vacuum cleaner
- ○ Lawnmower (if needed)
- ○ Curtains and blinds (if not included in sale)
- ○ First-aid kit
- ○ Extension leads
- ○ Cutlery
- ○ Pizza cutter
- ○ Blow-up mattress and sleeping bags (if you have no beds organised yet)
- ○ Towels
- ○ Teabags, coffee, sugar, milk, mug
- ○ Corkscrew and bottle opener
- ○ Pots and pans
- ○ Can opener, cheese grater, spatula, whisk, and any other kitchen implements.
- ○ Toaster
- ○ Kettle
- ○ Microwave
- ○ Iron and ironing board
- ○ Clothes horse

- ○ Clothes hangers
- ○ Laundry baskets
- ○ Dishwasher tablets
- ○ Washing detergent
- ○ Cling film/tinfoil
- ○ Matches and candles
- ○ Food for the first few nights
- ○ Batteries (AA, AAA, C, D and 9V)
- ○ Light bulbs (screw in and standard)
- ○ Bath/shower mat
- ○ Firelighters (if needed)
- ○ Tea towels and oven gloves
- ○ Cleaning supplies and gloves

Moving in is a stressful but very exciting time. Use this checklist to try and make sure you haven't forgotten anything but most importantly, enjoy the moment.

ACTION STEPS

- Have your checklist for items required to move.
- Transfer phone, broadband and TV services or shop around for new ones.

- Transfer TV licence.
- Redirect your mail.
- If moving out of a rental, make sure to:
  - Check the inventory
  - Clean the accommodation
  - Document the condition of the property, use photographs where possible
  - Pay any outstanding bills or charges, otherwise you risk losing part or all of your deposit

16
CHANGES TO IMPROVE THE HOME-BUYING PROCESS

IN this chapter, I will discuss some of the changes that could be made to the home-buying process in Ireland that would improve things for buyers, vendors, solicitors, and estate agents. These changes could result in greater transparency and clarity around the process, more efficient and effective communication between all parties, and a more streamlined and simplified approach to managing the various stages of the transaction. By implementing these changes, I think the home-buying process in Ireland would be a more positive and rewarding experience for everyone involved.

Sale-agreed contract

In my opinion, we should have a 'sale-agreed' contract in Ireland. We could bring in a new system under which, once a sale has been agreed upon between a buyer and a vendor, both parties would be legally bound to complete the transaction unless there are valid reasons for backing out. If either party chooses to withdraw from the sale without a valid reason, they would be required to pay fees to the other party to compensate for any expenses incurred as a result of the failed transaction. This would provide greater security and transparency for both buyers and vendors, and help reduce the risk of delays or setbacks in the home-buying process. Some examples of valid reasons for backing out of a sale might include issues with the property that were not disclosed during the sale process, or unforeseen financial difficulties that prevent the buyer from completing the transaction.

Pre-sale survey

Vendors should have to get the property surveyed by a registered surveyor to show up what issues the property has before it is allowed to be advertised for sale. A copy of the survey should then be given to people who plan on placing an offer on the home. They do this in Scotland and it results in more transparency and faster turnaround times. Often, sales fall through because of a survey turning up major structural issues. The home is then simply put back on the market, and the same thing happens again and again. It is a waste of everyone's time and money.

Communication

One solution to improve communication between buyers, vendors, solicitors and estate agents in the home-buying process could be to implement a project management tool that allows all parties to track the progress of the transaction and receive notifications when certain milestones are reached. This could include a centralised platform where all relevant documents and communications can be stored and accessed by all parties, as well as automated alerts and reminders when certain actions need to be taken. This type of tool could help to streamline the process and reduce the risk of miscommunication or delays.

Gazumping

Gazumping occurs when a property is sale-agreed and another party comes in and attempts to buy the home, sometimes by offering more money or sometimes by simply being a cash buyer and making a faster sale possible. This should be illegal and could be avoided by having a sale-agreed contract.

Legalities and probate

A home should not be allowed to be advertised for sale until all of its legalities are sorted, like probate or boundary issues. I think a home should only be allowed to be advertised for sale when it has no outstanding issues and keys are ready to be handed over once the process is complete.

Although this would initially delay a lot of homes coming to the market, over time it would improve the turnaround times when homes do go sale-agreed and would also improve the quality of property in the sales pool.

More transparency when bidding

One area where transparency could be improved in the home-buying process is during the bidding process. Currently, buyers may not have a clear understanding of how their bid compares to others, which can lead to frustration and a sense of uncertainty. This is one of the most common complaints I receive in my inbox.

One way to improve transparency during the bidding process could be to allow buyers to see the current highest bid and the number of other bids that have been placed, their increments and the times they were placed. This would give buyers a better sense of where they stand and allow them to make more informed decisions about whether to continue bidding or to walk away.

Some agents currently use third party online bidding platforms, while some have their own, but a centralised platform could be a great way of improving the process for everyone involved by providing a more transparent and efficient way for buyers to submit bids. It could provide real-time updates on the status of the bidding process by immediately emailing parties involved. For example, buyers could see the current highest bid and the number of other bids that have been placed, which would give them a better sense of where they stand and help them to make more informed decisions about whether to continue bidding or to walk away. Not only would this improve transparency for buyers and sellers, but it would remove a lot of time-consuming work for agents as they would no longer have to make individual phone calls or emails every time a new bid is placed.

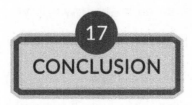

CONCLUSION

AND now, we have reached the conclusion of the book, but hopefully it is the beginning of your journey towards owning your very own piece of the Earth. By now you should be well-equipped with all the tips and tricks that I've accumulated over the years of running my Instagram page. And let me tell you, I've seen and heard it all. So, whatever challenges lie ahead, just know that you're not alone. I hope the good news stories scattered throughout the book help to keep you motivated and keep the end goal in mind.

You are now well-informed about the process of buying a home in Ireland, from mortgage approval to going sale-agreed. You are ready to take on the housing market with newfound confidence and knowledge. This journey may test your patience, persistence and sanity, but don't be discouraged by the hurdles you may encounter along the way. Embrace them as steps towards your end goal, and trust me, it will be worth it. When you turn the key in the door and spend that first night in your very own home, it's an incredible feeling that you will remember forever.

Good luck and happy house hunting!

Ciarán Mulqueen

ACKNOWLEDGEMENTS

I WANT to express my sincerest gratitude to my wife, Melissa, for her love and unwavering support throughout the writing of this book and the years prior. Her understanding, patience, and remarkable ability to handle everything going on in our family's lives is what allowed me to spend countless hours at the computer working on this book and my Instagram page (@crazyhouseprices). Without her, this would not have been possible. My family's encouragement and belief in me has also been immeasurable and I am eternally thankful for their support. I also want to thank my patrons and sponsors for their unwavering support of the page.

I am grateful to Outset Agency for their representation and to Hachette publishers for their expertise, guidance and dedication in making this book a reality. A special mention goes out to our one-year-old daughter Maisie, who brings so much joy to our lives and keeps me motivated to continue working hard. Thank you to everyone who has played a role in making this book a reality.

CHECKLIST FOR VIEWINGS

Below are some questions worth asking when viewing properties.

Property:

How flexible is the seller on the asking price?

_____

What is the energy rating?

_____

What aspect is the garden or balcony?

_____

_____

When was it built? (This could be important for home insurance, for example, it is often difficult to get home insurance on a home that is over 100 years old and may require a specialist insurer.)

_____

How is the property heated? Is it insulated?

_____

_____

Has the property or local area ever flooded? (This could be important for home insurance.)

_____

_____

_____

How old is the water boiler or water cylinder? When was it last serviced?

_____

If it was recently serviced, were there any follow-up repairs done?

_____

_____

What schools and transport links are available? (Google Maps should get you this information but local knowledge can be useful for schools.)

_____

_____

_____

How much will renovations cost?

_____

_____

Are the appliances part of the sale? If so, do they work? Do the windows open? Your surveyor should check these, along with taps, showers, toilets, but it's good to check yourself.

_____

_____

_____

CHECKLIST FOR VIEWINGS

Below are some questions worth asking when viewing properties.

Property:

How flexible is the seller on the asking price?

_____

_____

What is the energy rating?

_____

_____

What aspect is the garden or balcony?

_____

_____

When was it built? (This could be important for home insurance, for example, it is often difficult to get home insurance on a home that is over 100 years old and may require a specialist insurer.)

_____

_____

How is the property heated? Is it insulated?

_____

_____

Has the property or local area ever flooded? (This could be important for home insurance.)

_____

_____

_____

How old is the water boiler or water cylinder? When was it last serviced?

_____

_____

If it was recently serviced, were there any follow-up repairs done?

_____

_____

_____

What schools and transport links are available? (Google Maps should get you this information but local knowledge can be useful for schools.)

_____

_____

_____

How much will renovations cost?

_____

_____

Are the appliances part of the sale? If so, do they work? Do the windows open? Your surveyor should check these, along with taps, showers, toilets, but it's good to check yourself.

_____

_____

_____

CHECKLIST FOR VIEWINGS

Below are some questions worth asking when viewing properties.

Property:

How flexible is the seller on the asking price?

_____

_____

What is the energy rating?

_____

_____

What aspect is the garden or balcony?

_____

_____

When was it built? (This could be important for home insurance, for example, it is often difficult to get home insurance on a home that is over 100 years old and may require a specialist insurer.)

_____

_____

How is the property heated? Is it insulated?

_____

_____

Has the property or local area ever flooded? (This could be important for home insurance.)

_____

_____

_____

_____

How old is the water boiler or water cylinder? When was it last serviced?

_____

_____

If it was recently serviced, were there any follow-up repairs done?

_____

_____

_____

What schools and transport links are available? (Google Maps should get you this information but local knowledge can be useful for schools.)

_____

_____

_____

How much will renovations cost?

_____

_____

Are the appliances part of the sale? If so, do they work? Do the windows open? Your surveyor should check these, along with taps, showers, toilets, but it's good to check yourself.

_____

_____

_____

_____

CHECKLIST FOR VIEWINGS

Below are some questions worth asking when viewing properties.

Property:

How flexible is the seller on the asking price?

_____

_____

What is the energy rating?

_____

_____

What aspect is the garden or balcony?

_____

_____

When was it built? (This could be important for home insurance, for example, it is often difficult to get home insurance on a home that is over 100 years old and may require a specialist insurer.)

_____

_____

How is the property heated? Is it insulated?

_____

_____

Has the property or local area ever flooded? (This could be important for home insurance.)

_____

_____

_____

How old is the water boiler or water cylinder? When was it last serviced?

_____

_____

If it was recently serviced, were there any follow-up repairs done?

_____

_____

What schools and transport links are available? (Google Maps should get you this information but local knowledge can be useful for schools.)

_____

_____

_____

How much will renovations cost?

_____

_____

Are the appliances part of the sale? If so, do they work? Do the windows open? Your surveyor should check these, along with taps, showers, toilets, but it's good to check yourself.

_____

_____